Mike McGrath

HTML5

in
easy steps

In easy steps is an imprint of In Easy Steps Limited
Southfield Road · Southam
Warwickshire CV47 0FB · United Kingdom
www.ineasysteps.com

Notice of Liability
Every effort has been made to ensure that this book contains accurate
and current information. However, In Easy Steps Limited and the
author shall not be liable for any loss or damage suffered by readers
as a result of any information contained herein.

Trademarks
All trademarks are acknowledged as belonging to their respective
companies.

In Easy Steps Limited supports The Forest Stewardship Council (FSC),
the leading international forest certification organisation. All our titles
that are printed on Greenpeace approved FSC certified paper carry the
FSC logo.

MIX
Paper from
responsible sources
FSC® C020837

Printed and bound in the United Kingdom

ISBN 978-1-84078-425-1

Contents

Foreword

The creation of this book has been for me, Mike McGrath, an exciting personal journey in discovering how HTML5 can really be implemented in today's web browsers. Whereas my previous books on web page markup described all aspects of the finalized HTML 4.01 specifications it has been fascinating to determine exactly which parts of the (as yet) unfinalized HTML5 specifications are currently supported by Internet Explorer, Firefox, Google Chrome, Safari, and Opera. The "Handy Reference" section at the end of the book lists the working HTML5 tags and attributes. All the examples I have given in this book demonstrate HTML5 features that are presently supported by leading web browsers and the screenshots illustrate the actual results produced by the listed code. I truly believe that now, more than ever, authors can integrate HTML5 content markup, JavaScript functionality, and CSS presentation, to produce stunning interactive web pages.

Conventions in this book

In order to clarify the code listed in the steps given in each example I have adopted certain colorization conventions. Those parts of the HTML language itself are colored blue, like this:

<html>

Values assigned to HTML attributes are colored red, like this:

<html lang="en">

Literal content that is marked up by HTML tags is colored black, like this:

<title>HTML5 in easy steps</title>

Similarly, for style sheet code listed in the steps, those parts of the CSS language itself are colored blue and values assigned to properties are colored red, like this:

h1   { color : red ; background : yellow ; }

Additionally, in order to identify each source code file described in the steps a colored icon and the file name appears in the margin alongside the steps, such as these:

page.html   style.css   script.js   vector.svg   embed.pdf   audio.ogg   video.mp4

Grabbing the source code

For convenience I have placed all the source code files and associated files featured in this book into a single ZIP archive file, arranged in folders numbered to match the chapter numbers. You can obtain the complete archive by following these easy steps:

1 Browse to **http://www.ineasysteps.com,** then navigate to the "Resource Center" and choose the "Downloads" section

2 Find "HTML5 In Easy Steps" in the "Source Code" list, then click on the hyperlink entitled "All Code Examples" to download the archive

3 Now extract the archive contents to any convenient location on your computer

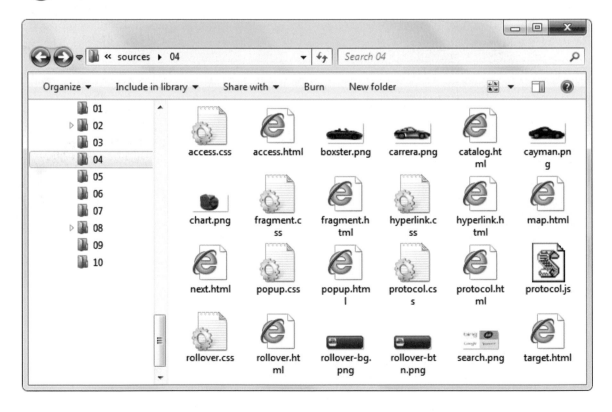

Undoubtedly HTML5 provides significant new creative possibilities in web page authoring - as I hope my examples demonstrate. I sincerely hope you enjoy discovering how HTML5 can be used to create stunning interactive web pages in today's latest web browsers as much as I did in writing this book.

Mike McGrath

1 Getting started

Welcome to the exciting world of the HTML5 web. This chapter introduces HTML5 and demonstrates how to create a "barebones" valid HTML5 document.

Introducing HTML5

The W3C is the recognized body that oversees standards on the web. See the latest developments on their informative website at **www.w3.org**.

Historically, the desire to have text printed in specific formats meant that original manuscripts were "marked up" with annotation to indicate to the book-printer how the author would like sections of text laid out. This annotation had to be concise and needed to be easily understood both by the printer and the author. A series of commonly recognized abbreviations therefore formed the basis of a standard markup language.

HyperText Markup Language (HTML) is a modern standard markup language that uses common abbreviations called "tags" to indicate to the web browser how the author would like to have sections of a web page laid out. It was first devised in March 1989 by British physicist Tim Berners-Lee at CERN in Switzerland (the European organization for nuclear research) to share all computer-stored information between the CERN physicists. Berners-Lee created a text browser to transfer information over the Internet using hypertext to provide point-and-click navigation. In May 1990 this system was named the World Wide Web and was enhanced in 1993 when college student Marc Andreessen added an image tag. Now that HTML could display both text and images the World Wide Web quickly became hugely popular.

Sir Tim Berners-Lee, creator of the World Wide Web.

As various web browsers were developed their makers began to add individual proprietary tags – effectively creating their own versions of HTML! The World Wide Web Consortium (W3C) standards organization recognized the danger that HTML could become fragmented so they created a standard specification to which all web browsers should adhere. This successfully encouraged the browser makers to support the standard tags. The W3C's HTML specification was continually revised to introduce new features until the publication of HTML version 4.01 at the turn of the century. At that time the W3C also published a specification for XHTML (eXtensible HTML), which strictly required all code to be "well-formed", to comply with the rules of eXtensible Markup Language (XML). This attempt to coerce web authors into adopting rigorous syntax, as Berners-Lee admits, did not work. So the W3C have returned to HTML and produced a draft specification, in consultation with all the browser makers, for version 5. The supported features of this version are described and demonstrated in this book, where it is generically referred to as "HTML5" or just plain "HTML".

What's new in HTML5?

Placing great emphasis on backward compatibility HTML5 is largely a superset of the previous version, but it introduces some great new features that let authors create more meaningful and exciting web pages:

- **<article>** – a structural element to contain stand-alone content, such as a self-contained topic

- **<section>** – a structural element to group together associated content, such as articles related to a common topic

- **<aside>** – a structural element to contain related supplemental content, such as a sidebar alongside a topic

- **<header>** – a structural element to contain page header content, such as a title and logo

- **<footer>** – a structural element to contain page footer content, such as copyright information and contact details

- **<ruby>** , **<rt>**, and **<rp>** – semantic elements to indicate pronunciation for East Asian languages, such as Japanese

- **<audio>** , **<video>**, and **<source>** – embedding elements to incorporate audio and video media that <u>does not</u> require external plug-ins, such as music files in MP3 format

- **<embed>** – an embedding element to incorporate media that <u>does</u> require an external plug-in, such as movies in SWF format

- **<canvas>** – an embedding element to create an area in which to dynamically draw bitmap graphics, such as graphs, games, and animations

Drawing on the area provided by the **<canvas>** element is accomplished exclusively using JavaScript and the new Canvas 2D API (Application Programming Interface). HTML5 also includes new DragNdrop, Web Storage, and Messaging APIs with which JavaScript can provide dynamic web page functionality.

Don't forget

Much effort has been made in HTML5 so that it does not "break the web" – by continuing to define how browsers should deal with legacy markup code.

Hot tip

HTML5 finally brings intrinsic support for audio and video content with codec support built into the browsers.

Addressing web pages

The World Wide Web comprises a series of large-capacity computers, known as "web servers", which are connected to the Internet via telephone lines and satellites. The web servers each use the HyperText Transfer Protocol (HTTP) as a common communication standard to allow any computer connected to any web server to access files across the web.

HTML web pages are merely plain text files that have been saved with a ".htm" or ".html" file extension, such as **index.html**.

In order to access a file across the web its web address must be entered into the address field of the web browser. The web address is formally known as its "Uniform Resource Locator" (URL) and typically has three parts:

Beware

A web page address (URL) cannot contain any blank spaces.

12

- **Protocol** – any URL using the HTTP protocol begins by specifying the protocol as **http://**

- **Domain** – the host name of the computer from which the file can be downloaded, For instance **www.example.com**

- **Path** – the virtual path to the file on the named domain, including any parent directory names where applicable. For instance **/htdocs/index.html**

A URL describing the location of a file by protocol, domain, and path is stating its "absolute address". So the absolute address of the file described by the protocol, domain, and path components above is **http://www.example.com/htdocs/index.html**.

Hot tip

Where an address states only the HTTP protocol and a domain name most web servers are configured to seek a file named **index.html** in their default directory.

Code contained within an HTML web page can reference other HTML files in any domain by their absolute address. HTML files resident within the same domain can also be referenced more simply by their "relative address", which means that files located within the same directory can be referenced just by their file name. For instance a file named "adjacent.html" located in the same directory can be referenced simply as **adjacent.html**.

Additionally, a relative address can reference a file within the parent directory by prefixing its name with "../". For instance a file named "higher.html" in the parent directory can be referenced from the current directory as **../higher.html**.

How do web servers work?

When you enter a URL into the browser address field the browser first examines the protocol. Where the protocol is specified as HTTP, or assumed to be HTTP if unspecified, the browser recognizes that a file is being sought from a web server. It then contacts a Domain Name Server (DNS) to look up the numerical Internet Protocol (IP) address of the specified domain name. Next a connection is established with the web server at that IP address to request the file at the specified path. When the file is successfully located it is copied back to the browser, otherwise the web server sends an error code, such as "404 – Page Not Found".

The Domain Name Server is typically run by your Internet Service Provider or by your company.

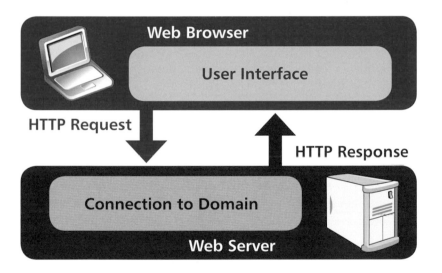

A successful response sends HTTP headers to the web browser, describing the nature of the response, along with a copy of the requested file. The HTTP headers are not normally visible but can be examined using various development tools, such as the Developer Tools feature in the Google Chrome browser:

Notice in the headers that the Content-Type is "text/html" – the MIME type used by all web servers to describe plain text HTML files.

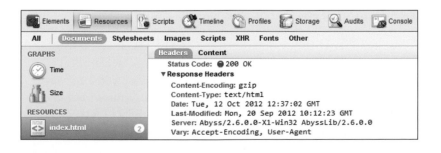

Defining document structure

The structure of an HTML5 document has these three parts:

- **Document type declaration** – declaring precisely which version of HTML is used to markup the document

- **Head section** – providing descriptive data about the document itself, such as the document's title and the character set used

- **Body section** – containing the content that is to appear when the document gets loaded into a web browser

Document type declaration

The document type declaration must appear at the start of the first line of every HTML5 document to ensure the web browser will "render" (display) the document in "Standards Mode" – following the HTML5 specifications. The document type declaration tag for all HTML5 documents looks like this:

<!DOCTYPE HTML>

It is important to note that HTML5 is not a case-sensitive language – so the document type declaration tag, and all other tags, may alternatively be written in any combination of uppercase and lowercase characters. For example, the following are all valid:

<!DOCTYPE html>

<!Doctype Html>

<!doctype html>

The choice of capitalization is yours but it is recommended you adhere consistently to whichever style you choose. The document type declaration tag capitalization style favored throughout this book uses all uppercase to emphasize its prominence as the very first tag on each page – but all other tags are in all lowercase.

Those familiar with previous versions of HTML may be surprised at the simplicity of the HTML5 document type declaration. In fact the document type declaration in previous versions was not actually part of the HTML language – so required lengthy references to schema documents. By contrast the HTML5 document type declaration is an intrinsic part of HTML itself.

Hot tip

The document type declaration in previous versions of HTML was part of the Standard Generalized Markup Language (SGML) from which HTML is derived.

...cont'd

The entire document head section and body section can be enclosed within a pair of **<html> </html>** tags to contain the rest of the document. The HTML5 specification actually states that these are optional but it is logical to provide a single "root" element. Most HTML tags are used in pairs like this to act as "containers" with the syntax **< tagname > data </ tagname >**.

Head section
The document's head section begins with an HTML opening **<head>** tag and ends with a corresponding closing **</head>** tag. Data describing the document can be added later between these two tags to complete the HTML document's head section.

Body section
The document's body section begins with an HTML opening **<body>** tag and ends with a corresponding closing **</body>** tag. Data content to appear in the browser can be added later between these two tags to complete the HTML document's body section.

Code comments
Comments can be added at any point within both the head and body sections between a pair of **<!--** and **-->** tags. Anything that appears between the comment tags is ignored by the browser.

Fundamental structure
So the markup tags that create the fundamental structure of every HTML5 document look like this:

```
<!DOCTYPE HTML>

<html>
 <head>
  <!-- Data describing the document to be added here -->
 </head>

 <body>
  <!-- Data content to appear in the browser to be added here -->
 </body>

</html>
```

Hot tip

An HTML "element" is any matching pair of opening and closing tags, or any single tag not requiring a closing tag – as described in the HTML5 element tags list on the inside front cover of this book.

Hot tip

The "invisible" characters that represent tabs, newlines, carriage returns, and spaces are collectively known as "whitespace". They may optionally be used to inset the tags for clarity.

Creating an HTML5 document

The fundamental HTML5 document structure, described on the previous page, can be used to create a simple HTML5 document in any plain text editor – such as Windows' Notepad application. In order to create a valid "barebones" HTML5 document information must first be added defining the document's primary written language, its character encoding format, and its title.

The document's primary language is defined by assigning a standard language code to a **lang** "attribute" within the opening **<html>** root tag. For the English language the code is **en**, so the complete opening root element looks like this: **<html lang="en">**.

The document's character encoding format is defined by assigning a standard character-set code to a **charset** attribute within a **<meta>** tag placed in the document's head section. The recommended encoding is the popular 8-bit Unicode Transformation Format for which the code is **UTF-8**, so the complete element looks like this: **<meta charset="UTF-8">**

Finally, the document's title is defined by text between a pair of **<title> </title>** tags placed in the document's head section.

Follow these steps to create a valid "barebones" HTML5 document:

Hot tip

The **<meta>** tag is a single tag – it does not have a matching closing tag. See the element tags list on the inside front cover of this book to find other single tags.

hello.html

Beware

HTML documents should not be created in word processors, such as MS Word, as they include additional information in their file formats.

1 Launch your favorite plain text editor then start a new document with the HTML5 document type declaration
<!DOCTYPE HTML>

2 Below the document type declaration, add a root element that defines the document's primary language as English
<html lang="en">
  <!-- Head and Body sections to be added here -->
</html>

3 Within the root element, insert a document head section
<head>
  <!-- Descriptive information to be added here -->
</head>

4 Within the head section, insert an element defining the document's encoding character set
<meta charset="UTF-8">

...cont'd

5 Next within the head section, insert an element defining the document's title
<title>Getting Started With HTML5</title>

6 After the head section, insert a document body section
<body>
  <!-- Actual document content to be added here -->
</body>

The quotation marks around an attribute value are usually optional but are required for multiple values. For consistency, attribute values in the examples throughout this book are all surrounded by quotation marks.

7 Within the body section, insert a size-one large heading
<h1>Hello World!</h1>

```
     hello.html
 1    <!DOCTYPE HTML>
 2
 3    <html lang="en">
 4
 5    <head>
 6     <meta charset="UTF-8">
 7     <title>Getting Started With HTML5</title>
 8    </head>
 9
10    <body>
11     <h1>Hello World!</h1>
12    </body>
13
14    </html>
```

17

8 Save the document as "hello.html", setting the encoding to the popular "UTF-8" format

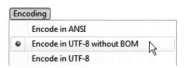

Encoding
  Encode in ANSI
  ● Encode in UTF-8 without BOM
  Encode in UTF-8

Windows' Notepad automatically adds a hidden "Byte Order Mark" (BOM) to the file while other editors (such as Notepad++ shown here) allow this to be omitted. Notepad++ can be freely downloaded from **notepad-plus-plus.org**.

9 Now open the HTML5 document in a modern web browser to see the title displayed on the title bar or tab, and the document content displayed as a large heading

← → | 🔍 hello.html | 🔍 ▾ → ✕ | 🔍 Getting Started With HTML5 ✕

Hello World!

Validating documents

Just as text documents may contain spelling and grammar errors, HTML documents may contain various errors that prevent them from conforming to the specification rules. In order to verify that an HTML document does indeed conform to the rules of its specified document type declaration it can be tested by a validator tool. Only HTML documents that pass the validation test successfully are sure to be valid documents.

The W3C's online HTML validator can be found at **validator.w3.org**.

Web browsers make no attempt at validation so it is well worth verifying every HTML document with a validator tool before it is published, even when the content looks fine in your web browser. When the browser encounters HTML errors it will make a guess at what is intended – but different browsers can make different interpretations so may display the document incorrectly. Conversely, valid HTML documents should always appear correctly in any standards-compliant browser.

The World Wide Web Consortium (W3C) provide a free online validator tool that checks the syntax of web documents:

 With an Internet connection, open your web browser and navigate to the W3C Validator Tool at **validator.w3.org** then click on the "Validate by File Upload" tab

Other tabs in the validator allow you to enter the web address of an HTML document located on a web server to "Validate by URI" or copy'n'paste all code from a document to "Validate by Direct Input".

2 Click the "Browse" button then navigate to the HTML document you wish to validate – once selected its local path appears in the validator's "File" field

3 Next click the validator's "Check" button to upload a copy of the HTML document and run the validation test – the result will then be displayed

Notice that the validator automatically detects the document's character set and HTML version.

If validation fails the errors are listed so you may easily correct them. When validation succeeds you may choose to include an icon at the end of the document demonstrating HTML5 support:

The HTML5 support logo is available in several sizes and formats – find more details online at **w3.org/html/logo**.

Employing an HTML editor

HTML code can be created in any plain text editor that provides encoding in the recommended UTF-8 format. As long as the code in the new text file is saved with a file extension of ".html" or ".htm" an HTML document is created. This file can then be opened in any web browser, such as Internet Explorer, to see how the HTML code is interpreted to "render" (display) the content on the screen.

Older web browsers, such as Internet Explorer 8 or earlier, will not fully recognize the modern HTML5 markup code. It is best therefore to view HTML5 web pages in the very latest version of Internet Explorer, Firefox, Google Chrome, Opera and Safari.

Some HTML authors prefer to use specialized HTML editors that colorize the various parts of the source code for greater clarity and offer further features. Microsoft's Expression Web editor, shown below, is a popular choice for many HTML authors.

Beware

The Expression Web interface also allows web pages to be created visually by dragging components onto its Design window – but knowledge of HTML is often helpful in fine-tuning the web page.

The Split view in Expression Web provides a live preview of what the HTML document will look like in a web browser. Additionally a built-in menu lets you quickly view the document in any web browser installed on your computer.

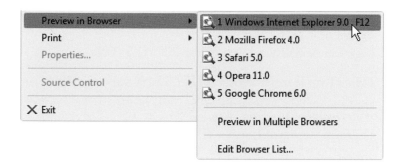

Don't forget

The W3C online validator tool can also be used to verify correct HTML code along with Expression Web's Compatibility Checker tool.

Expression Web's "Compatibility Checker" tool lets you easily locate code errors that do not conform to the declared document type. Additionally, like other Microsoft development tools, the Expression Web editor has "Intellisense", which identifies syntax errors live as you type the HTML code. This feature also provides context-sensitive menus that can insert HTML tags compatible with the current point in the document. For example, when you type a "<" in the head section Intellisense presents a list of tags that may be inserted at that point. After selecting a tag and typing a space Intellisense then presents a list of attributes that may be inserted within that tag.

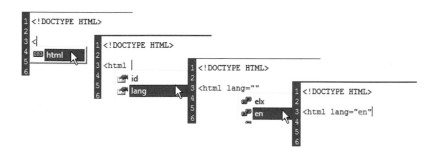

Hot tip

Expression Web also provides a customizable Code Snippet facility to quickly insert frequently used chunks of code – press **Ctrl+Enter** to see the Code Snippet list.

By default Intellisense automatically inserts a matching closing tag, if appropriate, whenever you type an opening tag. Some authors dislike this ability, however, but the Expression Web options allow Intellisense features to be turned on and off individually to customize the editor to your personal taste.

Summary

- The World Wide Web Consortium (W3C) is the recognized body that oversees standards on the web

- HTML5 introduces intrinsic support for audio and video media content

- JavaScript can draw on canvas areas and provide dynamic web page functionality using the new HTML5 APIs

- HyperText Transfer Protocol (HTTP) is the common communication standard used by web servers

- Uniform Resource Locator (URL) is an absolute web address comprising protocol, domain, and path components

- A relative address can reference an adjacent file by its file name and may use the syntax "../" to reference a parent directory

- Web servers send response headers back to the requesting computer and a copy of the file requested, or an error code

- Each HTML5 document should have a document type declaration, head section, and body section

- Information about the document itself is contained within the head section, and content is contained within the body section

- The document's written language is specified to the **lang** attribute in the opening **<html>** root element tag

- The document's character-set encoding is specified to the **charset** attribute in a **<meta>** tag, within the head section

- The document's title is specified between **<title>** **</title>** tags, within the head section

- The free online W3C validator tool should be used to verify that the HTML5 document is free of errors

- HTML5 documents can be created in a plain text editor or a specialized HTML editor such as Microsoft Expression Web

2

Providing page information

This chapter demonstrates how the head section of an HTML5 document can describe the document, incorporate scripts for functionality, and add style sheets for presentation.

Bestowing a title

The specifications require every HTML5 document to have a title, but its importance is often overlooked. The document title should be carefully considered, however, as it is used extensively:

- **Bookmarks** – save the document title to link back to its URL
- **Title Bar** – a web browser window may display the title
- **Navigation Tab** – a web browser tab may display the title
- **History** – saves the document title to link back to its URL
- **Search Engines** – read the document title and typically display it in search results to link back to its URL

You can find a chart of all character entities at **dev.w3.org/html5/html-author/charref.**

Document titles should ideally be short and meaningful – the task bar typically only displays 16 characters and tabs display around 32 characters.

Document titles throughout a website should follow a consistent naming convention and capitalize all major words. One popular naming convention provides a personal or company name and brief page description separated by a colon character. For example, "Amazon Books: HTML5 in easy steps". An alternative places the description first, so it remains visible when the title is truncated, and the name follows in brackets. For example, "HTML5 in easy steps [Amazon Books]".

Document titles, and document content, may contain special characters that are known in HTML5 as "entities". Each entity reference begins with an ampersand and ends with a semi-colon. For example, the entity **<** (less than) creates a "<" character and the entity **>** (greater than) creates a ">" character. These are often needed to avoid confusion with the angled brackets that surround each HTML tag. Other frequently used entities include ** ** (a single non-breaking space), **©** (©), **®** (®), and **™** (™). These are best avoided in document titles, however, as the vocal narrator used by visually impaired viewers may read each entity character as a word.

...cont'd

1 Start a new HTML5 with a document type declaration
`<!DOCTYPE HTML>`

title.html

2 Add a root element containing head and body sections
```
<html lang="en">
<head>
<!-- Data describing the document to be added here -->
</head>
<body>
<!-- Data content to appear in the browser
                              to be added here -->
</body>
</html>
```

3 Within the head section, insert a meta element specifying the character set and an empty title element
```
<meta charset="UTF-8">
<title> </title>
```

4 Within the title element insert a title including entities
`&lt; HTML5 in easy steps &gt;`

5 Save the document then open it in your web browser

6 Start a vocal narrator to hear the document title read out as "Less-than-HTML5-in-easy-steps-greater-than"

7 Edit the document title to make it more user-friendly
`&quot; HTML5 in easy steps &quote;`

8 Save the document once more then open it in your web browser to hear the narrator now read the document title as "HTML5 in easy steps"

Don't forget

The specifications do not define a naming scheme for document titles but do encourage authors to consider accessibility issues in all aspects of their web page designs.

Specifying a character set

The examples in this book are each saved files with Unicode encoding using the UTF-8 character-set. This character-set supports all characters in both Western and English languages, which allows the HTML document to contain characters from any language. Further character sets exist that also support all languages, while others exclusively support Western languages. The five most popular character-sets are listed below:

Don't forget

Character-set names are not case-sensitive – so "BIG5", "Big5", and "big5" are equivalent.

Name:	Character Set:
UTF-8	Multi-lingual Universal Transformation Format
BIG5	Multi-lingual traditional Chinese characters
SHIFT_JIS	Multi-lingual traditional Japanese characters
US-ASCII	US ASCII standard Western alphabet characters
ISO-8859-1	ISO standard Western alphabet characters

Although UTF-8 supports Chinese and Japanese characters they may appear as a simplified equivalent of those in the more specialized character sets, which create traditional characters.

1 Launch a text editor with Chinese language support and start with the HTML5 document type declaration
`<!DOCTYPE HTML>`

2 Add a root element containing head and body sections
```
<html lang="en">
<head> <!-- Information goes here --> </head>
<body> <!-- Content goes here --> </body>
</html>
```

3 Within the head section insert a meta element to specify the character set as BIG5, and add a document title
```
<meta charset="BIG5">
<title>BIG5 Encoding Example</title>
```

4 In the body section insert an English heading and its Chinese equivalent
```
<h1>Fantastic Web Page</h1>
<h1> 神乎其神 網頁 </h1>
```

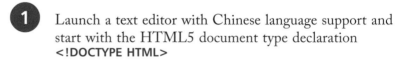

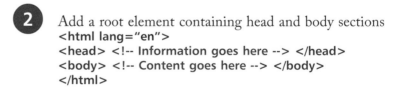

big5.html

5 Now save the document as "big5.html" – being sure to set the encoding to BIG5

6 Next recreate the HTML5 document, but this time specify the character set as UTF-8

utf-8.html

```
<!DOCTYPE HTML>
<html lang="en">
<head>
  <meta charset="UTF-8">
  <title>UTF-8 Encoding Example</title>
</head>
<body>
  <h1>Fantastic Web Page</h1>
  <h1> 神乎其神 網頁 </h1>
</body>
</html>
```

7 Save the second document as "utf-8.html" – being sure to set the encoding to UTF-8

8 Finally open both documents in your web browser and compare the appearance of the characters created by the two different character-set encodings

Hot tip

US ASCII was formerly the most commonly used encoding on the web, but it has now been surpassed by UTF-8 due to its wider support.

Refreshing the page

Meta information is simply data that describes other data. In the context of HTML, document meta data describes the document itself – rather than the document's contents.

HTML meta data is defined in the head section of the HTML document using the **<meta>** tag. Previous examples have used this tag to specify the document's character-set – as one piece of information describing that document. Further **<meta>** tags can be added to describe other aspects of the document.

The **<meta>** tag is an "empty" tag that needs no matching closing tag to create an HTML element. It is only used to specify information with its tag attributes. For example, its **http-equiv** attribute can represent a document HTTP header property and its **content** attribute specify that property's value.

Assigning the HTTP "refresh" property to a **<meta>** tag's **http-equiv** attribute can be used to reload the page after a number of seconds specified by its **content** attribute. For example, to reload the page after five seconds like this:

```
<meta http-equiv="refresh" content= "5">
```

This technique is often used on websites to dynamically update news or status items as it does not depend on JavaScript support. Another popular use redirects the browser to a new web page after a specified number of seconds like this:

```
<meta http-equiv="refresh" content= "5 ; url='new-page.html' ">
```

In this case the **<meta>** tag's **content** attribute specifies both the number of seconds to delay and the new URL to load.

refresh.html

1 Start with the HTML5 document type declaration
```
<!DOCTYPE HTML>
```

2 Add a root element containing head and body sections
```
<html lang="en">
<head>
<title>Refresh Example</title>
</head>
<body>
<h1>Moving in 5 Seconds...</h1>
</body>
</html>
```

28

3 Within the head section, insert meta elements to specify the encoding character set and refresh information

```html
<meta charset="UTF-8">

<meta http-equiv="refresh"
        content="5 ; url='new-page.html' ">
```

4 Save the document as "refresh.html" then create the HTML document to which the browser will re-direct

```html
<!DOCTYPE HTML>
<html lang="en">
<head>
<meta charset="UTF-8">
<title>Refresh Example - New</title>
</head>
<body>
<h1>Moved Here After 5 Seconds!</h1>
</body>
</html>
```

new-page.html

5 Save the second document as "new-page.html", in the same directory as "refresh.html", then open the first document in your browser to see the browser get re-directed after a five second delay

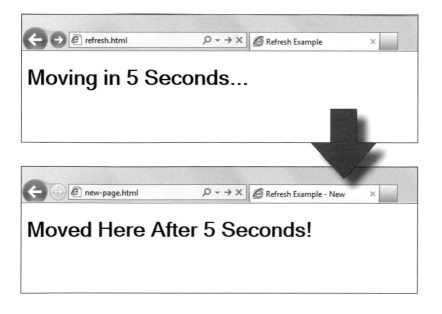

Hot tip

Notice that the **content** attribute value entirely surrounds both the delay and URL with double quote marks, but the URL is just surrounded by single quote marks.

Describing the document

In addition to specifying the document's character-set and expiry date **<meta>** tags can be used to provide descriptive information that may be useful to search engines. This offers no guarantee of high ranking however, as search engines also use other page information for that purpose – especially the document title. Nevertheless it is helpful to provide a description and a list of keywords relevant to the contents of that page so that search engine "spiders" might usefully add the page to their index.

Descriptive **<meta>** tags always have a **name** attribute, to specify a page feature, and a **content** attribute to specify that feature's value. For example, the "description" name allows you to specify text content describing the page. This should be short succinct sentences that might appear in a search engine's results page. Any description longer than around 200 characters may get truncated.

Similarly, the "keywords" name allows you to specify text content in the format of a comma-separated list of relevant keywords. These may be used by search engines to influence their results. For example, a search for "italian ceramics" could return all web pages with "italian" and "ceramics" in their keywords list. Promotion of the web page by keywords is best achieved by following some simple guidelines:

- Use only lowercase characters

- Keep all keywords on a single line

- Never repeat a keyword in a list

- Limit the keywords list to 1,000 characters or less

- Try to use the plural form for keywords – to match searches made with both the single and plural forms of that word

To specify that a web page should not by indexed by search engines the "robots" name should have a content value of "noindex". Conversely, this may be set to "all" to explicitly allow indexing, but as that is the default state it's not really necessary.

...cont'd

1 Start with the HTML5 document type declaration
<!DOCTYPE HTML>

keywords.html

2 Add a root element containing head and body sections
<html lang="en">
<head>
  <title>Tuscan Home Decor [Italian Ceramics]</title>
</head>
<body> <h1>Beautiful Tuscan Ceramics</h1> </body>
</html>

Hot tip

Notice that the first four meta keywords in this example also appear in the meta description.

3 Within the head section, insert meta elements to specify the encoding character-set, description, and keywords
<meta charset="UTF-8">

<meta name="description"
content="Shop for beautiful Italian Ceramics,
                Tuscan Majolica, Home Decor, and more.">

<meta name="keywords"
content="tuscan,italian,ceramics,home decor,majolica,
                dinnerwares,vases,plates,bowls">

31

4 Save the document then open it with Firefox and use the Page Info dialog on the context menu to see the meta data

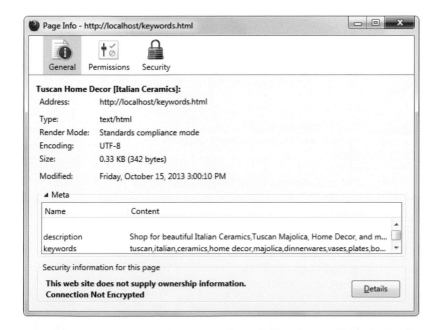

Hot tip

There are a number of free meta tag generators available online – enter "free meta tag generator" into a search engine.

Incorporating scripts

Scripts can be incorporated within HTML documents to interact with the user and to provide dynamic effects. This ability has become increasingly important with the development of Web 2.0 pages in which sections of the page can be dynamically updated. Previously the browser would typically request an entire new page from the web server, which was less efficient and more cumbersome, so Web 2.0 is a great improvement.

Scripts enclosed by **<script> </script>** tags can be added within the head section of an HTML document but, in line with the aim of HTML5 to separate content from presentation, are best contained in a separate file. The **<script>** tag automatically assumes a **type** attribute value of **"text/javascript"** as scripts are expected to use the JavaScript language by default. This means that the **type** attribute can be omitted from the tag unless you are incorporating a script that uses a different scripting language. The URL of the script file must be assigned to a **src** attribute within the **<script>** tag when incorporating an external script. For example, add an adjacent script file named "script.js" like this:

<script src="script.js"></script>

Alternative fallback content can be provided in the document's body section between **<noscript></noscript>** tags, which will only be displayed when script functionality is absent or disabled.

script.html

1 Start with the HTML5 document type declaration
<!DOCTYPE HTML>

2 Add a root element containing head and body sections
<html lang="en">
<head>
** <meta charset="UTF-8">**
** <title>JavaScript Example</title>**
</head>
<body>
** <h1>Static</h1> <h1>Dynamic</h1>**
</body>
</html>

3 In the head section, insert an element to incorporate an external JavaScript file
<script src="script.js"> </script>

4 In the body section, insert a fallback message
`<noscript>JavaScript Not Enabled!</noscript>`

5 Save the HTML5 document then open a new text editor
window and copy this script, exactly as it is listed

```
function init()
{
  var h1tags = document.getElementsByTagName("h1") ;
  h1tags[1].onclick = react ;
}

function react()
{
  this.innerHTML = "Clicked!" ; this.style.color = "red" ;
}
onload = init ;
```

script.js

6 Save the JavaScript file as "script.js" in the same directory
as the HTML5 document then open the web page in
your browser and click on the second heading

Hot tip

You can learn more
about scripting with
"JavaScript In Easy Steps".

This script attaches a behavior to the second heading element so
when it gets clicked by the user its text content and color change.

33

Incorporating style sheets

Style sheets can be incorporated within HTML documents to control the presentational aspects of each element on the page. The use of style sheets has replaced all features of HTML that formerly related to presentation. For example, the **<font>** tag has become obsolete as font family, weight, style, and size are now specified by a style sheet rule.

Style sheets enclosed by **<style> </style>** tags can be added within the head section of an HTML document to enclose rules governing how the content will appear. The **<style>** tag automatically assumes a **type** attribute value of **"text/css"** as style sheets are expected to use the Cascading Style Sheet language by default. This means that the **type** attribute can be omitted from the tag unless you are incorporating a style sheet that uses a different styling language. For example, a simple style sheet containing rules to determine the appearance of all size-one headings could look like this:

<style>

h1 { color : red ; background : yellow ; }

</style>

This is acceptable and will validate but, in line with the aim of HTML5 to separate content from presentation, style sheets are best contained within a separate file. The great advantage of placing style sheets, and scripts, in separate files is that they can be applied to multiple HTML documents – thus making website maintenance much easier. Editing a shared style sheet or script instantly affects each HTML document that shares that file.

An external style sheet is incorporated within an HTML document by adding a **<link>** tag in the document's head section. This must contain a **rel** (relationship) attribute assigned a **"stylesheet"** value, and the URL of the style sheet must be assigned to its **href** attribute. Once again this tag automatically assumes a **type** attribute value of **"text/css"** for style sheets so the **type** attribute can be omitted unless you are incorporating a style sheet that uses a different styling language. For example, add an adjacent style sheet file named "style.css" like this:

<link rel="stylesheet" href="style.css">

Hot tip

The **<link>** tag is a single tag – it does not have a matching closing tag. See the element tags list on the inside front cover of this book to find other single tags.

...cont'd

1 Start with the HTML5 document type declaration
<!DOCTYPE HTML>

style.html

2 Add a root element containing head and body sections
```
<html lang="en">
<head>
  <meta charset="UTF-8">
  <title>Style Sheet Example</title>
</head>
<body>
  <h1>Styled Heading</h1>
</body>
</html>
```

3 Within the head section, insert a link to an adjacent style sheet file
<link rel="stylesheet" href="style.css">

4 Save the HTML document then open a new text editor window and precisely copy this style sheet
```
h1
{
        color : red ;
        background : yellow ;
        border : 10px dashed blue ;
        padding : 5px ;
        width : 550px ;
}
```

style.css

5 Save the Cascading Style Sheet file in the same directory as the HTML5 document then open the web page in your browser to see the style rules applied

Coloring the **<h1>** element without setting a **width** rule would reveal that it occupies the entire width of the browser window – except for the default margins of the body.

Linking more resources

The <link> tag that was used in the previous example to incorporate a style sheet in an HTML5 document can also be used to incorporate other resources into a document.

This tag may only appear in the head section of a document but the head section can contain many <link> tags. Each <link> tag must contain **rel** and **href** attributes, stating the relationship and location respectively, together with a **type** attribute where appropriate to specify the MIME type of the linked resource.

Permitted rel (relationship) values:				
alternate	archives	author	bookmark	external
first	help	icon	index	last
license	next	nofollow	noreferrer	pingback
prefetch	prev	search	stylesheet	sidebar
tag	up			

Many of the link types above are intended to help search engines locate resources associated with that HTML document and the <link> tag may also include a **title** attribute to further describe the resource. For example a version of the page in another language:

<link rel="alternate" type="text/html" href="esp.html"
title="Esta página en Español - This page in Spanish" >

In this case the location of the resource is specified using a relative address that, by default, the browser will seek in the directory in which the HTML document is located. The browser can, however, be made to seek a relative address in a different directory by inserting a <base> tag at the start of the document's head section. Its **href** attribute can then specify the absolute directory address. For example, to specify a separate "resources" directory like this:

<base href= "http://localhost/resources/">

It is popular to link an icon resource to display in the web browser's address field. This can be placed in a directory specified by the <base> tag for most browsers but Internet Explorer insists the icon is located in the web server's root directory and named exactly as "favicon.ico". All browsers do, however, recognize all other resources in the directory specified by the <base> tag.

1 Start with the HTML5 document type declaration
<!DOCTYPE HTML>

link.html

2 Add a root element containing head and body sections
```
<html lang="en">
<head>
  <meta charset="UTF-8">
  <title>Link Example</title>
</head>
<body>
  <h1>Linked Icon</h1>
</body>
</html>
```

3 Within the head section, insert elements to specify a base "resources" directory and an icon resource
```
<base href="http://localhost/resources/">
<link rel="icon" href="cubes.ico">
```

4 Save the HTML document then open an icon editor, such as IcoFX, and create an icon sized 16x16 pixels

5 Now save the icon in the "resources" directory named as "cubes.ico", and also save a copy in the root directory named precisely as "favicon.ico" – for Internet Explorer

6 Open the HTML document in your web browser via a web server to see the icon resource appear in the address field

This page is served to the browser by a local web server using the default "localhost" domain. Simply opening a local copy of this example in a browser will not display the icon.

Summary

- A document title is used by search engines and may be seen in a browser's title bar, navigation tab, bookmarks, and history

- Document content and titles can include character entity references to display special characters, such as **©** for ©

- Character-sets that support Eastern language characters often also support Western language characters

- A **<meta>** tag can be used to refresh the page at a specified interval or to redirect the browser to a different page

- Search engine spiders can use the keywords and description specified in **<meta>** tags to add a web page to their index

- A keywords list should comprise only non-repeating lowercase keywords on a single line of the HTML document

- Scripts can be added to the head section of an HTML5 document between **<script> </script>** tags but are best created in a separate file for incorporation by this tag's **src** attribute

- Style sheets can be added to the head section of an HTML5 document between **<style> </style>** tags but are best created in a separate file for incorporation by a **<link>** tag

- Editing a shared script or shared style sheet instantly affects each HTML document that shares that file – making website maintenance much easier

- A **<link>** tag may only appear in the head section of an HTML document and must contain **rel** and **href** attributes to describe the resource's relationship and location

- A **<base>** tag can be added at the start of the head section to specify a particular directory in which to seek relative addresses

- An icon link type can incorporate an icon named **favicon.ico** that may appear in the browser window and on favorite lists

3 Creating body content

This chapter demonstrates how text and image elements can be created within the body section of an HTML5 document.

Working the body

Every HTML5 document should contain exactly one opening **<body>** tag and exactly one matching closing **</body>** tag – defining the body section to contain all document content that is intended for display in the web browser window.

The body section of a HTML document should not contain any meta data, scripts, or style sheets – **<meta>**, **<script>**, and **<link>** elements all belong in the head section.

Uniquely the opening **<body>** tag may contain attributes to reference the "load" event that occurs when the page has completely loaded in the web browser, and the "unload" event that occurs when leaving that page or when closing the browser. These **onload** and **onunload** attributes are useful when scripting to respond to the load and unload page events.

The **onload** attribute references the same load event that was used in the example on page 33 to create an "event-handler" function. Within the **<body>** tag the **onload** attribute can specify the name of a script function to call when the load event occurs. Similarly the **onunload** attribute can specify a script function to be called when the unload event occurs.

Alternatively short script "snippets" can simply be assigned to the attributes within the HTML **<body>** tag. For example, the **onload** attribute could call upon the intrinsic **alert()** function to launch an alert dialog whenever that page gets loaded. This function can specify a message to be displayed by the dialog as a text string within quotes between the function parentheses. With entire attribute values surrounded by double quotes it is important to enclose the message text string within single quotes to avoid terminating the attribute value prematurely, like this:

```
<body onload= "alert( 'Greetings!' )" >
```

If double quotes were used throughout in the example above the attribute value would become **"alert("**. This principle of differentiating text strings must be applied to any attribute value that contains a "nested" quote.

The **onunload** attribute can call upon the intrinsic **alert()** function to display a message in an alert dialog in the same way.

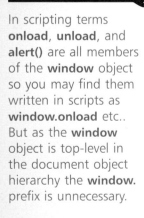

Don't forget

Scripts and style sheets are best contained in separate files and incorporated into the HTML document by **<script>** and **<link>** elements placed within its head section.

40

Hot tip

In scripting terms **onload**, **unload**, and **alert()** are all members of the **window** object so you may find them written in scripts as **window.onload** etc.. But as the **window** object is top-level in the document object hierarchy the **window.** prefix is unnecessary.

...cont'd

1 Start with the HTML5 document type declaration
```
<!DOCTYPE HTML>
```

body.html

2 Add a root element containing head and body sections
```
<html lang="en">
<head>
  <meta charset="UTF-8">
  <title>Body Attributes Example</title>
</head>
<body>
  <h1>Page Loaded</h1>
</body>
</html>
```

3 Now insert attributes to specify event-handlers for the load and unload events
```
<body onload="alert( 'Greetings!' )"
      onunload="alert( 'Goodbye!' )" >
```

4 Save the HTML document then open it in your web browser to see the alert dialog appear when it has loaded

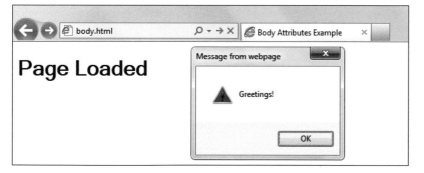

5 Click OK to close the alert dialog then navigate to a different page, close the web browser, or refresh the page to see the alert dialog appear when the document gets unloaded

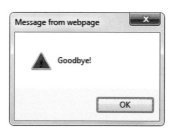

Hot tip

The **onload** and **onunload** attributes are remnants from earlier versions of HTML. It is better to specify event-handler functions in a script file – in line with the aim of HTML5 to separate content from presentation.

Inserting paragraphs

All text content is traditionally separated into sentences and paragraphs to be more easily read and more readily understood. This is also true for text content in HTML5 documents and their paragraphs are contained within **<p> </p>** tags. Each paragraph element is visually separated from the next one by the browser – typically leaving two empty lines between them.

Text within a paragraph will normally automatically wrap to the next line when it meets the element's edge but it can be forced to wrap sooner by inserting a line break **
** tag.

For emphasis a horizontal rule **<hr>** tag can be inserted between paragraphs to draw a line separating them. The **<hr>** tag cannot, however, be inserted inside a paragraph to separate sentences. You may be surprised to find the **<hr>** tag in HTML5 as it would seem to perform a purely presentational function. It is however described in the specifications as representing a "paragraph-level thematic break", such as a scene change in a story.

The **
** tag and **<hr>** tag are both single tags that need no matching closing tag.

para.html

1 Start with the HTML5 document type declaration
<!DOCTYPE HTML>

2 Add a root element containing head and body sections
<html lang="en">
<head>
  <meta charset="UTF-8">
  <title>Paragraph Example</title>
</head>
<body>
  <!-- Heading and paragraphs to be inserted here -->
</body>
</html>

3 Insert a large heading within the body section
<h1>The Statue of Liberty</h1>

4 Next add a paragraph within the body section
<p>The Statue of Liberty was built over nine years by French sculptor Auguste Bartholdi.Upon its completion in 1884 all 350 individual pieces of the statue were packed into 214 crates for the long boat ride from France to New York.</p>

5 After the paragraph, add a horizontal ruled line
`<hr>`

6 After the horizontal ruled line, add a second paragraph
`<p>`The statue arrived in the America several months later and was reconstructed on Liberty Island. Auguste Bartholdi thought that the New York harbor was the perfect setting for his masterpiece because it was where immigrants got their first view of the New World.`</p>`

7 Now insert breaks into the paragraphs to control the length of their lines
`<p>`The Statue of Liberty was built over nine years by French sculptor Auguste Bartholdi.`<br>`Upon its completion in 1884 all 350 individual pieces of the statue were packed into `<br>`214 crates for the long boat ride from France to New York.`</p>`

`<p>`The statue arrived in the America several months later and was reconstructed on `<br>`Liberty Island. Auguste Bartholdi thought that the New York harbor was the perfect `<br>`setting for his masterpiece because it was where immigrants got their first view of `<br>`the New World.`</p>`

8 Save the HTML document then open it in your web browser to see the heading, paragraphs, forced line breaks, and horizontal ruled line

The **`<hr>`** element can be considered to be the HTML equivalent of the *** section separator often found in stories and essays.

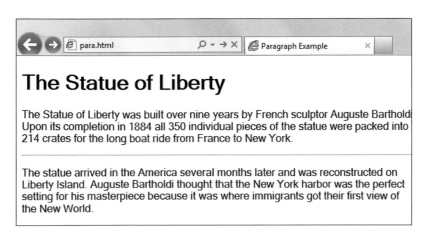

Including quotations

It is important to recognize that some HTML5 elements produce a rectangular block area on the page in which to display content, while others merely produce a small block on a line within an outer containing block. These are referred to as "flow" and "phrasing" elements. Phrasing elements, which produce a small block on a line, must always be enclosed by a flow element, which produces the larger containing block, such as **\<p> \</p>**. The difference between flow elements and phrasing elements can be seen by contrasting how web browsers display the two HTML elements that are used to include quotations in documents.

The **\<blockquote> \</blockquote>** tags are intended to surround long quotations from another source, which can be specified by its **cite** attribute. For this element the browser typically produces a rectangular block area to contain the quotation, starting on a new line and indented from surrounding content – so **\<blockquote>** is a flow element.

The **\<q> \</q>** tags on the other hand are intended to surround short quotations from another source, which can be specified by its **cite** attribute. For this element the browser typically produces a small block area on the current line to contain the quotation – so **\<q>** is a phrasing element.

Unlike the **\<blockquote>** flow element, the **\<q>** phrasing element causes the browser to automatically add quotation marks around the element's content when it gets displayed on the page. Ideally these should be double quotation marks surrounding the entire element content and single quotation marks around any inner nested quotations, but its implementation may vary.

quote.html

1 Start with the HTML5 document type declaration
\<!DOCTYPE HTML>

2 Add a root element containing head and body sections
```
<html lang="en">
<head>
  <meta charset="UTF-8">
  <title>Quotation Example</title>
</head>
<body>
 <p>A Paragraph Flow Block!</p>
</body>
</html>
```

...cont'd

3 Within the body section insert a blockquote containing two small nested quotations

```
<blockquote cite="http://www.example.com/origin.html">
A Blockquote Flow Block!<br>Paul said, <q>I saw Emma
at lunch, she told me <q>Susan wants you to get some
ice cream on your way home.</q> I think I will get some
at Ben and Jerry's on Main Street.</q> </blockquote>
```

5 Save the HTML document then open it in different browsers to compare the quotation implementations

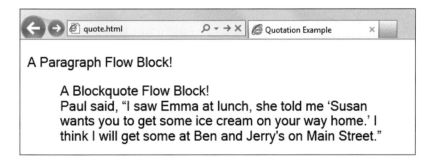

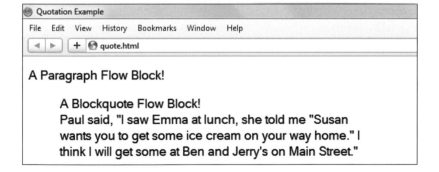

Adding styles to the elements reveals their block areas:

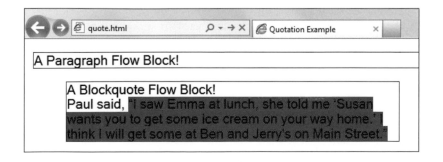

Emphasizing text

HTML5 provides four phrasing elements that can be used to emphasize text within the body of a document:

- Text enclosed between **<b> </b>** tags is enhanced without conveying extra importance, such as keywords in a paragraph – typically displayed in a bold font

- Text enclosed between **<i> </i>** tags is enhanced without conveying extra importance, such as technical terms in a paragraph – typically displayed in an italic font

- Text enclosed between **<strong> </strong>** tags gains increased importance, without changing the meaning of the sentence – typically displayed in a bold font

- Text enclosed between **<em> </em>** tags should be stressed to deliberately affect the meaning of the sentence – typically displayed in an italic font

It is perhaps surprising that the **<b>** and **<i>** tags remain in HTML5 as they outwardly suggest that content should be presented in a bold or italic font – contradicting the aim of HTML5 to separate structure from presentation. According to the specifications their meaning has been redefined, however, so content within a **<b>** element should be "stylistically offset" and that within an **<i>** element should be seen as in an "alternate voice". In real terms these are nonetheless represented by bold and italic fonts but should only be used as a last resort as they do not convey meaning – use **<strong>** and **<em>** tags instead.

The advantage of the **<strong>** and **<em>** tags is that they describe the importance of their content relative to surrounding text and let the browser choose how it should be presented. Additionally these tags are more relevant to suggest how narrators should convey their content vocally.

As with many HTML tags the **<strong>** and **<em>** tags can be nested but care must be taken to close nested elements correctly. For example, **<strong><em>...</em></strong>** is the correct order, whereas **<strong><em>...</strong></em>** is incorrect and will not validate.

Don't forget

The specifications encourage web page authors to consider accessibility issues in all aspects of their web page designs.

...cont'd

1 Start with the HTML5 document type declaration
`<!DOCTYPE HTML>`

emphasis.html

2 Add a root element containing head and body sections
```
<html lang="en">
<head>
  <meta charset="UTF-8">
  <title>Emphasis Example</title>
</head>
<body>
 <!-- Document content to be added here -->
</body>
</html>
```

3 Within the body section, add a paragraph that emphasizes some text without affecting the meaning of the sentence
```
<p><strong>Warning.</strong> This dungeon is
dangerous.<strong>Avoid the ducks.</strong> Take
any gold you find.<strong>Do not take any of the
diamonds,they are explosive.</strong> You have been
warned.</p>
```

4 Next within the body section, add paragraphs that emphasize some text to affect the meaning of the sentence
```
<p><em>Puppy dogs</em> are cute.</p>
<p>Puppy dogs <em>are</em> cute.</p>
<p>Puppy dogs are <em>cute.</em></p>
```

5 Save the HTML document then open it in your web browser to see how the text has been emphasized

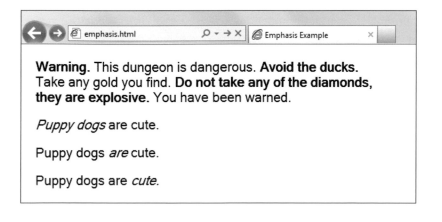

Hot tip

The `<b>` tag should be avoided wherever possible but one legitimate use is to markup the lead sentence of an article.

47

Reading the small print

HTML5 provides three elements that can be used to fomat text within the body of a document:

- Text enclosed between **<small> </small>** tags is regarded as a side comment to surrounding text, such as copyright information – typically displayed in a smaller font

- Text enclosed within **<del> </del>** tags is regarded as having been removed from the document, such as a completed item in a "to do" list – typically displayed with a strikethrough line

- Text enclosed within **<ins> </ins>** tags is regarded as having been added to the document, such as a new additional item in a "to do" list – typically displayed with an underline

The **<small>** tag is only meant to contain short comments that supplement surrounding content. It is not intended for use with large sections of text, such as multiple paragraphs, as that would be considerably more than a side comment.

In displaying content contained within a **<small>** element the web browser considers the size of the font used to display the surrounding content then applies an appropriate reduction. Therefore, where the surrounding content is displayed with a font of 12-point size, content contained within a **<small>** element might be displayed with a font of 10-point size – the precise size is determined by the browser.

Both **<del>** and **<ins>** elements can be used within a section of content, to markup snippets of changed text, and to enclose entire sections of changed content, such as replaced paragraphs.

format.html

1 Start with the HTML5 document type declaration
```
<!DOCTYPE HTML>
```

2 Add a root element containing head and body sections
```
<html lang="en">
<head>
  <meta charset="UTF-8"><title>Format Example</title>
</head>
<body> <!-- Content to be added here --> </body>
</html>
```

3 Within the body section, insert a paragraph containing a side comment for legal purposes
`<p>Example Corp today announced record profits for the second quarter <small>(Full Disclosure: EG News is a subsidiary of Example Corp)</small>, leading to speculation about a merger with Demo Group.</p>`

4 Next insert a large heading and a regular paragraph
`<h1>To Do List</h1>`
`<p>Empty the dishwasher</p>`

5 Now insert a paragraph that has been deleted
`<del><p>Take out the trash</p></del>`

6 Then insert a paragraph that has been added
`<ins><p>Sweep the yard</p></ins>`

7 Finally insert a paragraph that has been added, which contains a text snippet that has been changed
`<ins>`
`<p>Feed the <del>dog</del><ins> cat</ins></p>`
`</ins>`

8 Save the HTML document then open it in your web browser to see how the text has been formatted

The **\<big>** and **\<tt>** tags in the previous version of HTML are now obsolete as they were seen as presentational.

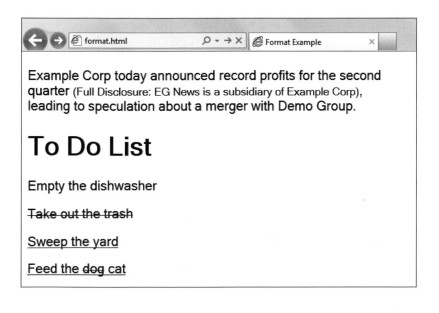

Example Corp today announced record profits for the second quarter (Full Disclosure: EG News is a subsidiary of Example Corp), leading to speculation about a merger with Demo Group.

To Do List

Empty the dishwasher

~~Take out the trash~~

Sweep the yard

Feed the ~~dog~~ cat

The **\<small>** tag does not denote content of lesser importance, only that it is a side comment to surrounding text.

Keeping preformatted text

Where it is desirable to have the browser render text content that has been "preformatted" the web page author can enclose that content between **<pre> </pre>** flow element tags. These advise the browser that the following instructions should be applied:

● Preserve white space

● Render all text with a fixed-width font

● Disable automatic word-wrapping

● Do not disable bi-directional processing

Preserving the white space retains all spaces, tabs, and line breaks. This is great to display lengthy poems in which every second line is indented. For example, with this verse:

```
ReadingGaol.txt - Notepad
File   Edit   Format   View   Help
In Debtors' Yard the stones are hard,
    And the dripping wall is high,
So it was there he took the air
    Beneath the leaden sky,
And by each side a Warder walked,
    For fear the man might die.
```

In this case each second line is indented by four character widths – created by hitting the space bar four times to insert four invisible space characters. These indents will be exactly preserved by the **<pre>** element as four character widths.

Tab characters, on the other hand, can present some surprises as they are usually interpreted by a browser as eight character widths. This agrees with the tab size in Windows' Notepad application but other text editors can vary. This means that preformatted text containing tab characters may appear to be mis-aligned by the **<pre>** element. It is for this reason that the specifications discourage the use of tab characters when creating preformatted text content.

The **<pre> </pre>** tags can also be useful to ensure "Text-Art", sometimes used as web forum signatures, will appear as intended.

Beware

Use spaces rather than tabs when preparing preformatted text.

...cont'd

1 Start with the HTML5 document type declaration
<!DOCTYPE HTML>

2 Add a root element containing head and body sections
<html lang="en">
<head>
<meta charset="UTF-8">
<title>Preformat Example</title>
</head>
<body> **<!-- Content to be added here -->** **</body>**
</html>

3 Within the body section, insert a document heading
<h1>Text-Art Signature</h1>

4 Ensure that the font in your text editor is set to a fixed width font, such as Lucida Console for Notepad

5 Next in the body section, insert a **<pre>** element containing preformatted content in a fixed width font – and produced without any tab characters
<pre>

```
           ----      @
     ----     _`‾\(,_
     ----  (*)/ (*)        MIKE'S PUSHBIKES
~~~~~~~~~~~~~~~~~~~~~~~~~~~~~~~~~~~~~~~~~~~~~~~
```
</pre>

6 Save the HTML document then open it in your web browser to ensure the content retains preformatting

preformat.html

51

Modifying text

Regular text in a paragraph area of a web page is displayed in invisible inline phrasing boxes that comprise an outer logical box, and an inner font box containing a baseline:

An inline phrasing box.

Logical box
Baseline
Font box

The vertical line spacing is determined by the font height to allow space between characters that extend below the baseline, such as "p", and tall characters that extend upwards, such as "b", plus a vertical margin area.

> Text in a paragraph written in an inline phrasing box.
> Lines are spaced so characters do not collide. ™

Additionally the font box will accommodate "superscript", such as the trade mark symbol ™ produced by the **™** character entity. Superscript is any text, number, or symbol that appears smaller than regular text and is set above the baseline. Mathematical formulae can use superscript to indicate numeric powers with the character entities **²** for ^{2} and **³** for ^{3}. The font box will also accommodate "subscript" – that appears smaller than regular text and is set below the baseline.

The height available for superscript and subscript with the standard vertical line spacing is limited so the character size is restricted. Rather than use character entities for this purpose it is often better to use the HTML5 **** tags for superscript and **** tags for subscript. These elements increase the vertical line spacing to allow more prominent superscript and subscript characters. For example, **²** is larger than **²**. Additionally any content can be included within these elements so you are not restricted to available character entity references.

> Lines are spaced so characters do not collide with the superscript below.
> Text line in a paragraph containing ^{superscript} and $_{subscript}$
> Lines are spaced so characters do not collide with the subscript above.

You can find a chart of all character entities at **dev.w3.org/html5/html-author/charref**.

...cont'd

1 Start with the HTML5 document type declaration
```
<!DOCTYPE HTML>
```

modify.html

2 Add a root element containing head and body sections
```
<html lang="en">
<head>
  <meta charset="UTF-8">
  <title>Modify Text Example</title>
</head>
<body> <!-- Content to be added here --> </body>
</html>
```

3 Within the body section, insert a paragraph containing superscript produced by character entities
```
<p>Square of four: 4&sup2; = 16 <br>
      Cube of four: 4&sup3; = 64</p>
```

4 Now in the body section, insert a similar paragraph containing superscript produced by HTML elements
```
<p>Square of four: 4<sup>2</sup> = 16 <br>
      Cube of four: 4<sup>3</sup> = 64</p>
```

5 Finally in the body section, insert a paragraph containing subscript produced by HTML elements
```
<p>Water: H<sub>2</sub>O <br>
      Oil of Vitriol: H<sub>2</sub>SO<sub>4</sub>
</p>
```

6 Save the document then open it in your browser to compare the superscript and to see the subscript text

53

Hot tip

When using superscript [2] in paragraphs to denote area, such as 10 feet^2, you may prefer to use the entity **²** rather than **²** to keep line spacings equal.

Displaying code in text

HTML5 provides three phrasing elements specifically to display computer program code within the body of a document:

● Complete program code, or program snippets, can be enclosed between **<code> </code>** tags for display in a suitable font

● Program variable instances can be enclosed between **<var> </var>** tags to differentiate them from regular text

● Sample program input and output can be enclosed between **<samp> </samp>** tags to differentiate them from regular text

The contact address for the source of the program code can also be provided between **<address> </address>** flow element tags.

code.html

1 Start with the HTML5 document type declaration
<!DOCTYPE HTML>

2 Add a root element containing head and body sections
```
<html lang="en">
<head>
  <meta charset="UTF-8">
  <title>Program Code Example</title>
</head>
<body> <!-- Content to be added here --> </body>
</html>
```

Note that all angled bracket characters in the program code have been replaced by character entities to avoid conflict with the HTML tags.

3 In the body section, insert preformatted program code
```
<pre>
<code>
#include &lt;iostream&gt;
using namespace std;

int main()
{
  float degF, degC;
  cout &lt;&lt; "Enter Fahrenheit Temperature: ";
  cin &gt;&gt; degF;
  degC = ((degF - 32.0 ) * (5.0 / 9.0));
  cout &lt;&lt; degF &lt;&lt; "F is " &lt;&lt; degC &lt;&lt; "C";
  cout &lt;&lt; endl;
  return 0;
}
</code>
</pre>
```

4 Now in the body section, insert a program description containing variables, sample input, and sample output
<p>
This program assigns an input value to <var>degF</var>
then performs a conversion on that value, assigning the
result to <var>degC</var> for output.
For example, input of <samp>98.6</samp>
will output <samp>37C</samp>.
</p>

5 Next in the body section, state the program code source
<address>From:<q>C++ Programming in easy steps</q>
at www.ineasysteps.com</address>

6 Save the HTML document then open it in your web browser to see how the program code, description, and source details appear

---

```
                code.html              🔍 ▾ → ✕   Program Code Example    ✕


#include <iostream>
using namespace std;

int main()
{
  float degF, degC;
  cout << "Enter Fahrenheit Temperature: ";
  cin >> degF;
  degC = ((degF - 32.0 ) * (5.0 / 9.0));
  cout << degF << "F is " << degC << "C";
  cout << endl;
  return 0;
}


This program assigns an input value to degF then performs a
conversion on that value, assigning the result to degC for output.
For example, input of 98.6 will output 37C.

From:"C++ Programming in easy steps" at www.ineasysteps.com
```

Don't forget

Remember to insert the phrasing **<code>** element within a **<pre>** flow element to preserve the program code layout in an HTML document.

Giving tooltip advice

HTML5 provides four phrasing elements that can be used to designate advisory phrases within the body of a document:

- Text can be enclosed between **<abbr> </abbr>** tags to indicate it is an abbreviation

- Text can be enclosed between **<cite> </cite>** tags to indicate it is a citation or reference from another source

- Text can be enclosed between **<dfn> </dfn>** tags to indicate it is the definitive instance of that term

- Text can be enclosed between **<kbd> </kbd>** tags to indicate input to be entered by the user from the keyboard

Every HTML5 element that can legally appear within the body of a document may optionally include a **title** attribute. Values specified to a **title** attribute are typically displayed as a tooltip that pops up when the user places the cursor over the element. This means that each of the phrasing elements listed above can include a **title** attribute to expand on the meaning of its content.

advice.html

1 Start with the HTML5 document type declaration
<!DOCTYPE HTML>

2 Add a root element containing head and body sections
```
<html lang="en">
<head>
  <meta charset="UTF-8">
  <title>Advice Example</title>
</head>
<body> <!-- Content to be added here --> </body>
</html>
```

3 In the body section, insert a paragraph containing an abbreviation with tooltip advice
```
<p><abbr title="HyperText Markup Language">HTML
</abbr>5 in easy steps</p>
```

4 Next insert a citation reference with tooltip advice
```
<p><cite title="Inventor of the HyperText Markup
Language">Sir Tim Berners-Lee</cite></p>
```

5 Now insert a definitive term with tooltip advice
```
<p><dfn title="The popular language of the
WorldWideWeb. Commonly abbreviated to 'HTML'">
HyperText Markup Language</dfn></p>
```

6 Then insert a keyboard instruction with tooltip advice
```
<p><kbd title="Press the Y key on your keyboard to
execute a script. This requires JavaScript to be enabled in
your browser">Hit Y to Continue.</kbd></p>
```

Remember to use single quote marks for nested quotes – as with 'HTML' in step 5.

7 Finally add an element in the head section to identify a script that will respond to the keyboard instruction
```
<script src="advice.js"> </script>
```

8 Save the HTML document, then exactly copy the script below and save it as "advice.js" alongside the HTML file
```
function showkey(e) {
var obj= ( navigator.appName ===
              "Microsoft Internet Explorer") ? event : e ;
if( obj.keyCode === 89 || obj.keyCode === 121 )
              alert( "Y pressed. Thank You." ) ;
}
document.onkeydown = showkey ;
```

advice.js

9 Open the HTML document and place the cursor over the elements to see the individual tooltips

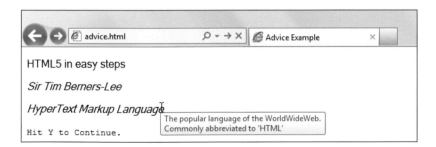

Hot tip

The script looks at the keycode when the key gets pressed and will respond to lowercase "y" and uppercase "Y".

10 With JavaScript support enabled in your browser, press the Y key to see the script response

Adding images

The ability to add images to HTML document content introduces lots of exciting possibilities. An image is easily added to the document using the **<img>** tag, which should preferably always include these attributes:

- A **src** attribute is required to specify the image location URL, by either its absolute or relative path

- A **width** attribute is recommended to specify the pixel width of the area the image will occupy on the page

- A **height** attribute is recommended to specify the pixel height of the area the image will occupy on the page

- An **alt** attribute is recommended to specify text describing the image, for occasions when the image cannot be loaded

The values assigned to the **width** and **height** attributes instruct the web browser to create a content area on the web page of that size. This need not be the actual dimensions of the image as the web browser can render the image in another specified size. Care must be taken to avoid distortion by ensuring the dimensions are scaled in proportion to the actual image size. Additionally images should only be scaled down as scaling up often results in pixelation – where individual pixels are visible to the eye. It is inefficient, however, to rely upon the browser to scale images that are not to be displayed full size as this requires downloading unnecessarily larger files. It is better to adjust the image size to the actual dimensions it will occupy on the web page using a graphics editor, such as Photoshop, so it will download and display faster.

58

Original file size

fish.png

Item type: PNG File
Dimensions: 600 x 449
Size: 124 KB

Reduced to 33%

fish.png

Item type: PNG File
Dimensions: 200 x 150
Size: 30.5 KB

The optimum file type for web bitmap graphics is the popular non-proprietary Portable Network Graphics (PNG) format, which produces compact files and supports transparency.

...cont'd

1 Start with the HTML5 document type declaration
<!DOCTYPE HTML>

image.html

2 Add a root element containing head and body sections
```
<html lang="en">
<head>
  <meta charset="UTF-8"> <title>Image Example</title>
</head>
<body> <!-- Content to be added here --> </body>
</html>
```

3 Within the body section, insert three image elements – to display a graphic at full size plus two scaled versions
```
<img src="fish.png" width="200" height="150"
                    alt="Goofy Fish Image Large">
<img src="fish.png" width="150" height="112"
                    alt="Goofy Fish Image Medium">
<img src="fish.png" width="100" height="75"
                    alt="Goofy Fish Image Small">
```

4 Save the document then open it in your browser to see the background shining through transparent image areas

Hot tip

To change Internet Explorer's default background color select Tools, Internet Options, General, Colors, uncheck Use Windows Colors, then click Background and choose a new color.

Directing languages

The recommended UTF-8 document encoding format provides support for bi-directional text, so that characters from languages written right-to-left, such as Hebrew, are automatically written in that direction and may appear alongside left-to-right text such as English. Additionally HTML5 provides a **<bdo>** bi-direction override element to which a text direction can be explicitly specified as either "ltr" or "rtl" by its **dir** attribute.

The bi-direction override allows characters from right-to-left languages to be written as character entities in an HTML document in "logical" left-to-right order, but to be displayed in "visual" right-to-left order. For example, the **<bdo>** element below encloses five character entities from left-to-right, in the order they may have been entered, but displays them right-to-left:

<bdo dir="rtl">ישראל</bdo>

.... appears as ישראל (Yiśrā'ēl in the Latin alphabet).

For Eastern languages HTML5 supports "ruby annotation" that usefully provides pronunciation alongside text. In Japanese, for example, there is more than one alphabet. Text written in the semantic "kanji" alphabet, which has thousands of characters, is often annotated with its equivalent in the phonetic "hiragana" language, which has around fifty characters, to aid pronunciation. This is called "furigana" in Japanese and "ruby" in English - named after the small font used to indicate the pronunciation.

For the benefit of Westerners, the Japanese kanji text can be annotated with "romaji" – its Latin alphabet equivalent. Similarly in Chinese, text written in the "mandarin" alphabet can be annotated with "pinyin" – its Latin alphabet equivalent.

HTML5 ruby annotation first encloses the main text between **<ruby> </ruby>** tags. These tags may then enclose the pronunciation between **<rt> </rt>** (ruby text) tags after the main text. Supporting browsers display the pronunciation above the main text, but non-supporting browsers display both side-by-side.

Surrounding the entire **<rt>** element with parentheses between **<rp> </rp>** (ruby parentheses) tags displays the pronunciation in parentheses after the main text in non-supporting browsers, while cleverly continuing to display the pronunciation (without parentheses) above the main text in supporting browsers.

...cont'd

ruby.html

1 Start with the HTML5 document type declaration
```
<!DOCTYPE HTML>
```

2 Add a root element containing head and body sections
```
<html lang="en">
<head>
  <meta charset="UTF-8"> <title>Ruby Example</title>
</head>
<body> <!-- Content to be added here --> </body>
</html>
```

3 In the body section, insert an element for Japanese text
```
<ruby>東京</ruby>
```

4 Within the ruby element, add pronunciation annotation
```
<ruby>東京 <rt>tō kyō</rt></ruby>
```

5 Now surround the pronunciation with ruby parentheses
```
<rp> (</rp> <rt>tō kyō</rt> <rp>)</rp>
```

6 Next insert a complete ruby element for Chinese text
```
<ruby>北京
<rp> (</rp> <rt>běi jīng</rt> <rp>)</rp>
</ruby>
```

7 Save the document then open it in different browsers to compare how the ruby annotations get displayed

Hot tip

The ruby elements are illustrated with an added border style for clarity.

Summary

- The **<body>** element encloses all document content and its opening tag may include **onload** and **onunload** attributes

- A paragraph is enclosed within a **<p>** element and may use the **
** tag to force breaks between lines of text

- Flow elements create a block area on the page in which to display content, phrasing elements create a small block on a line within the outer containing block

- Long quotations may be enclosed within a **<blockquote>** flow element and short quotations within a **<q>** phrasing element

- The **<em>** and **<strong>** phrasing elements are preferred over the **<b>** and **<i>** phrasing elements to emphasize text

- Side comments can be enclosed within a **<small>** element and the **<ins>** and **<del>** elements used to indicate replaced text

- To avoid mis-alignment tab spacing should be avoided when creating preformatted text for inclusion within a **<pre>** element

- Superscript and subscript can be included using character entities or using the **<sup>** and **<sub>** elements

- Program code can be included in a HTML document using the **<code>**, **<var>** and **<samp>** elements, and a contact address for the source provided within an **<address>** element

- The **<abbr>**, **<cite>**, **<dfn>**, and **<kbd>** elements provide advice

- Most elements that can appear in the document body can include a **title** attribute to provide Tooltip text

- The **<img>** tag places an image on the web page and should preferably always include **src, width, height,** and **alt** attributes

- Text display direction can be explicitly specified by the **dir** attribute in a **<bdo>** element

- Ruby annotation uses the **<ruby>**, **<rt>** and **<rp>** elements to provide pronunciation aid for Eastern languages

4 Inserting hyperlinks

This chapter demonstrates how to insert hyperlinks in an HTML5 document so the user can navigate around the web page or site.

Creating hyperlinks

When the internet carried only text content "hypertext" provided the ability to easily access related documents and was fundamental to the creation of the world wide web. Today images can also be used for this purpose so any navigational element of a web page is now referred to as a "hyperlink".

Hyperlinks are enclosed between **<a> </a>** anchor tags, which specify the target URL to an **href** (hyperlink reference) attribute in the opening tag. The web browser will display a hyperlink in a manner that distinguishes it from regular text – typically hypertext gains an underline and image-based hyperlinks gain a colored border.

Each web page hyperlink is sensitive to three interactive states:

- **Hover** – gaining focus, the cursor is placed over the hyperlink

- **Active** – retrieving the linked resource, the user clicks the link

- **Visited** – the linked resource has previously been retrieved

Style rules can be used to emphasize each hyperlink state:

hyperlink.html

1 Start with the HTML5 document type declaration
<!DOCTYPE HTML>

2 Add a root element containing head and body sections, with a link element pointing to a style sheet
```
<html lang="en">
<head>
<meta charset="UTF-8">
<title>Hyperlink Example</title>
<link rel="stylesheet" href="hyperlink.css">
</head>
<body>  <!-- Content to go here --> </body>
</html>
```

3 Within the body section, insert a hyperlink to a target page, including tootip advice
```
<a href="target.html"
title="A hyperlink to a target page">Visit Target</a>
```

...cont'd

4 Save the HTML document then create a similar second document containing a link targeting the first document
`<a href="hyperlink.html"`
`title="A hyperlink to return">Return</a>`

target.html

5 Save the second HTML document then create a style sheet to emphasize each hyperlink state
`a:hover  { background : yellow ; }`
`a:active  { background : lime ;   }`
`a:visited { background : aqua ;   }`

hyperlink.css

6 Save the style sheet then open the first web page in your browser to see the hyperlink in its default state

7 Place the cursor over the hyperlink to see its hover state, then hold down the left mouse button to see the hyperlink's active state

Don't forget

The hyperlink on the target page instantly appears in the visited state because the browser recognizes that its return target has been previously visited.

8 Now release the mouse button to load the linked target resource, then click its hyperlink to reload the first document and see that hyperlink's visited state

Accessing links via keys

There are three ways to access the target of a hyperlink:

- **Pointer** – a mouse, trackball, or similar device places a screen pointer over a hyperlink then the user clicks to access its target

- **Tab** – repeatedly hit the Tab key to successively focus on each hyperlink in turn, then hit Return to access the target of the currently selected hyperlink

- **Access Key** – hit a designated character key to focus on a particular hyperlink, then hit Return to access its target

A designated character key is specified for a hyperlink by the **accesskey** attribute of an **<a>** anchor tag. The method to utilize the designated key varies across browsers – Windows users must press ALT+*accesskey* with Internet Explorer, Google Chrome, or Safari, but press ALT+SHIFT+*accesskey* with Firefox, and press SHIFT+ESC, then *accesskey* with Opera.

access.html

1 Start with the HTML5 document type declaration
<!DOCTYPE HTML>

2 Add a root element containing head and body sections, with a link element pointing to a style sheet
<html lang="en">
<head>
<meta charset="UTF-8">
<title>Access Example</title>
<link rel="stylesheet" href="access.css">
</head>
<body> <!-- Content to go here --> </body>
</html>

3 Within the body section, insert two hyperlinks that designate different numeric access key characters
<a href="access.html" accesskey="1">Home Page</a> |
<a href="catalog.html" accesskey="2">Catalog Page</a>

catalog.html

4 Save the HTML document then create a similar second document containing the same two hyperlinks
<a href="access.html" accesskey="1">Home Page</a> |
<a href="catalog.html" accesskey="2">Catalog Page</a>

5 Save the second HTML document, then create a style
sheet to remove the default hyperlink styles and to
highlight each hyperlink when they receive focus

```
a        { text-decoration : none ; color : black ; }
a:focus { background : red ; color : white ; }
```

access.css

6 Now save the style sheet then open the first web page in
your browser to see the hyperlinks without default styles

Beware

Removing the default
hyperlink styles means
they are no longer easily
recognizable as links – so
it is best avoided unless
some other indication
makes the user aware
they can be used for
navigation purposes.

7 Hit the Tab key repeatedly until the second hyperlink
receives focus, then hit Return to follow that link

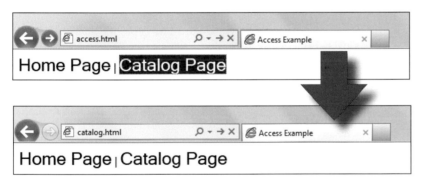

67

8 Press the appropriate access key combination for your
browser and number 1 key, such as ALT+1 for Internet
Explorer, then hit Return to follow the first hyperlink

Hot tip

Mac users should press
CMD+*accesskey* with
their Safari browser.

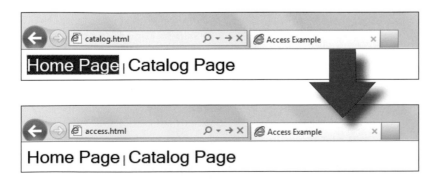

Linking to page fragments

Hyperlinks can target a specific point in a document that has been created with a "fragment" identifier – an element with a unique identifying name assigned to an **id** attribute in its opening tag. Within the hyperlink, the fragment identifier is specified to a **href** attribute in the opening **<a>** tag prefixed by a # hash character. For example, the tag **<a href="#top">** targets an element within the same document that contains the unique fragment identifier name of "top".

A hyperlink can also target a specific point in a different document using the document's URL, followed by a # hash character, then the fragment identifier. For example, the tag **<a href="index.html#top">** targets an element within a document named "index.html" that contains the unique fragment identifier name of "top".

Following a hyperlink to a fragment identifier displays the document from the point where the fragment identifier appears:

fragment.html

1 Start with the HTML5 document type declaration
<!DOCTYPE HTML>

2 Add a root element containing head and body sections, with a link element pointing to a style sheet
<html lang="en">
<head>
<meta charset="UTF-8">
<title>Fragment Example</title>
<link rel="stylesheet" href="fragment.css">
</head>
<body> <!-- Content to go here --> </body>
</html>

3 Within the body section, insert two hyperlinks that contain fragment identifiers and also target different fragments
<a id="top" href="#btm">Skip to Page Foot</a> |
<a id="next-btm" href="next.html#btm">
                              Skip to Next Page Foot</a>

4 Next in the body, insert a content paragraph followed by a hyperlink containing a fragment identifier and targetting the first hyperlink in the document
<p class="yellow-block"></p>
<a id="btm" href="#top">Skip to Page Head</a>

Don't forget

The # hash character is used in HTML to target fragments and to specify hexadecimal color values, and in CSS to select elements by their **id** attribute for styling.

68

...cont'd

5 Save the HTML document then create a second similar document with hyperlinks both above and below content

```
<a id="top" href="#btm">Skip to Page Foot</a>
<p class="red-block">Content...</p>
<a id="btm" href="#top">Skip to Page Head</a> |
<a id="prev-top" href="fragment.html#top">
                      Skip to Previous Page Head</a>
```

next.html

6 Create a style sheet that sizes and colors the content area of each document – representing different page bodies

```
p.yellow-block   { height : 700px ; background : yellow ; }
p.red-block      { height : 700px ; background : red ; }
```

fragment.css

7 Save the style sheet then open the first web page in your browser and follow the hyperlinks to each of this document's fragments below and above its body content

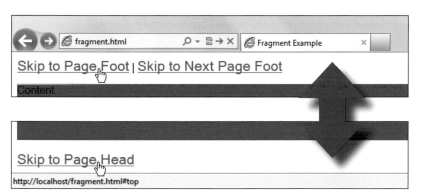

8 Now follow the hyperlink to the fragment in the second document, then return to top of the first document

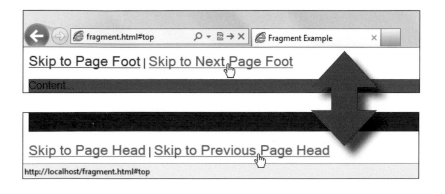

Hot tip

At the end of lengthy pages include a hyperlink to a fragment at the top of the page so the user need not scroll back up.

Linking to protocols

The **href** attribute of a hyperlink will typically target a resource using the HyperText Transfer protocol **http:** but it may also target resources using other protocols. Script functions can be called with the **javascript:** protocol and email clients can be invoked by the **mailto:** protocol:

protocol.html

1 Start with the HTML5 document type declaration
<!DOCTYPE HTML>

2 Add a root element containing a head section, incorporating a style sheet and script, and a body section
```
<html lang="en">
<head>
<meta charset="UTF-8">
<title>Protocol Example</title>
<link rel="stylesheet" href="protocol.css">
<script src="protocol.js"></script>
</head>
<body>  <!-- Content to go here -->  </body>
</html>
```

3 Within the body section, insert an image and a paragraph containing two hyperlinks that target different protocols
```
<img id="chart" src="chart.png" alt="Chart Image">
<p id="links">
<a href="javascript:toggle()">Show/Hide Chart</a>  <br>
<a href="mailto:wendy@example.com">Email Wendy</a>
</p>
```

protocol.css

4 Save the HTML document then create a style sheet with a rule to hide the image and a rule to style the paragraph
```
img#chart { visibility : hidden ; height : 0px ; }
p#links { padding : 5px ;
          border : 3px double green ; width : 200px ; }
```

protocol.js

5 Save the style sheet then create a script to alternately reveal and hide the image when the first hyperlink gets activated
```
function toggle()
{
  var tag = document.getElementById( "chart" ) ;
  var hid = ( tag.style.visibility !== "visible" ) ;
  tag.style.visibility = ( hid ) ? "visible" : "hidden" ;
  tag.style.height = ( hid ) ? "auto" : "0px" ;
}
```

...cont'd

6 Save the script, then open the web page in your browser and click on the first link to reveal the image element

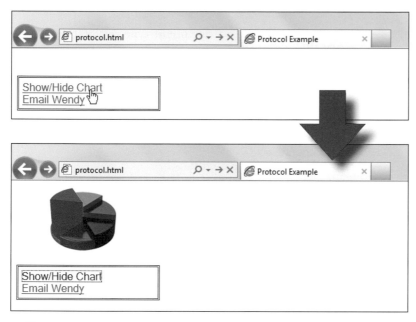

Hot tip

This script first examines the current visibility status of the image element, then reverses it.

7 Click on the first hyperlink to hide the image element again, then click on the second hyperlink to launch your default client email application – ready to send a message

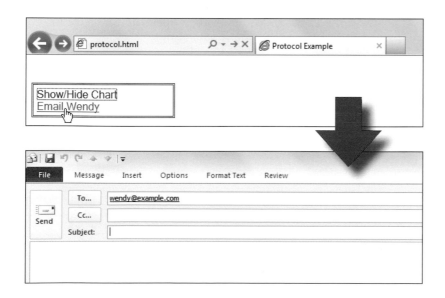

Don't forget

The **mailto:** protocol automatically adds the email address of the recipient in the "To" field of the email client.

Using images as hyperlinks

To make the navigational features of an HTML document more visually appealing images can be used as hyperlinks – simply by nesting an **<img>** element within an **<a>** hyperlink element:

rollover.html

1 Start with the HTML5 document type declaration
<!DOCTYPE HTML>

2 Add a root element containing head and body sections, with a link element pointing to a style sheet
<html lang="en">
<head>
<meta charset="UTF-8">
<title>Rollover Example</title>
<link rel="stylesheet" href="rollover.css">
</head>
<body> <!-- Content to go here --> </body>
</html>

3 Within the body section, insert a paragraph containing a hyperlink with a nested image of a specific size
<p class="btn">
<a href="http://www.youtube.com">
<img src="rollover-btn.png"
**   alt="Hyperlink to YouTube" width="192" height="67" >**
</a>
</p>

4 Save the HTML document then open the web page in your browser and follow the hyperlink

The dimensions of this button are exaggerated for illustration purposes – web page buttons are typically smaller.

...cont'd

Browsers usually add a border around an image when it is nested within a hyperlink to indicate that it is not merely an illustration. Style rules can remove the image border and can also swap the image when the cursor is placed over it to perform a "rollover". There are several ways to achieve this effect – the technique described below hides the image when the cursor is placed over it to reveal the background image on the container element behind:

5 Create a style sheet beginning with a rule to set the paragraph container element the same size as the button image and to specify the container's background image
p.btn { width : 192px ; height : 67px ;
     background : url(rollover-bg.png) ; }

6 Next add a style rule to set the nested hyperlink element to the same size as the button image
p.btn a { display : block ; width : 192px ; height : 67px ; }

7 Now add a style rule to remove the default border from around the nested button image element
p.btn a img { border : 0px ; }

8 Finally add a style rule to hide the button image when the cursor is placed over it
p.btn a:hover img { visibility : hidden ; }

9 Save the style sheet then open the web page in your browser to see the border removed and the rollover effect

rollover.css

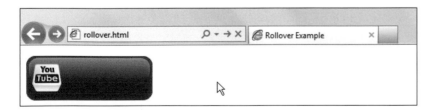

Hot tip

Unlike some other rollover techniques here both images are already loaded, so the rollover performs instantly – and the **<img>** tag provides alternative text when images are disabled.

Producing image map links

A single image can target multiple hyperlink resources if an image "map" is added to define "hot spot" areas for each hyperlink. To use an image map the **<img>** tag must include a **usemap** attribute to specify a map name, prefixed by a **#** hash character. The image map itself is contained between **<map> </map>** tags and its name is specified by a **name** attribute in the opening **<map>** tag.

Each area of the image that is to become a hyperlink hot spot is defined by four attributes of an **<area>** tag within the **<map>** element. The **shape** attribute specifies its shape as **rect** (rectangle), **circle**, or **poly** (polygon), and the **coords** attribute specifies a comma-separated list of its x-axis and y-axis coordinates:

Shape:	Coordinates:
rect	top-left x, top-left y, bottom-right x, bottom-right y
circle	center x, center y, radius
poly	x1,y1,x2,y2,x3,y3,etc. – one pair for each point. The first and final point must have identical coordinates to complete the shape

Additionally each **<area>** tag must have an **href** attribute, to specify the hyperlink's URL target, and an **alt** attribute to specify alternative text to be displayed when images are not enabled.

map.html

1 Start with the HTML5 document type declaration
<!DOCTYPE HTML>

2 Add a root element containing head and body sections
<html lang="en">
<head>
<meta charset="UTF-8">
<title>Image Map Example</title>
</head>
<body> <!-- Content to go here --> </body>
</html>

3 Within the body section, insert an image and map element
<img src="search.png" alt="Search" usemap="#search">
<map name="search"> <!-- Areas to go here --> </map>

4 Within the map element, define a rectangular hot spot covering the top left quarter of the image – from a top left point at xy:0,0 to a bottom right point at xy:200,100

```
<area   shape="rect" coords="0,0,200,100"
            href="http://www.bing.com"
            alt="Bing Panel" title="Link to Bing">
```

5 Now in the map element, define three hot spots of the same size covering the other three quarters of the image

```
<area   shape="rect" coords="200,0,400,100"
            href="http://www.ask.com"
            alt="Ask Panel" title="Link to Ask">

<area   shape="rect" coords="0,100,200,200"
            href="http://www.google.com"
            alt="Google Panel" title="Link to Google">

<area   shape="rect" coords="200,100,400,200"
            href="http://www.yahoo.com" alt="Yahoo Panel"
            title="Link to Yahoo">
```

6 Save the HTML document, then open the web page in your browser to see the Tooltips describe each hot spot that you can follow to open its associated target resource

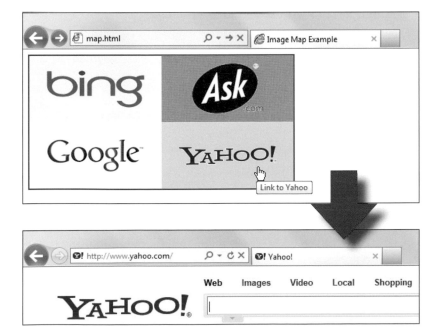

Do not leave any spaces in the comma-separated list of coordinates.

search.png 400px x 200px

75

Validation will fail unless each **<area>** tag includes an **alt** attribute.

Generating popups

Hyperlinks can also be used without an actual target resource to perform both CSS rollovers and "popup" effects. Typically the hyperlink's **<a>** anchor tag **href** attribute will specify a **#null** value in this case. The CSS **a:hover** psuedo-class can create hot spots – much like the image map hot spots in the previous example. In response the style rules can reveal previously hidden HTML elements to be displayed as popups in front of other content. These are useful to display additional graphical or text content:

popup.html

1 Start with the HTML5 document type declaration
<!DOCTYPE HTML>

2 Add a root element containing head and body sections, with a link element pointing to a style sheet
```
<html lang="en">
<head>
<meta charset="UTF-8">
<title>PopUp Example</title>
<link rel="stylesheet" href="popup.css">
</head>
<body>  <!-- Content to go here --> </body>
</html>
```

3 Within the body section, insert a paragraph containing hyperlinks with nested image elements
```
<p id="models">
<a href="#null">Cayman
<img class="pop" src="cayman.png" alt="Cayman">
</a>

<a href="#null">Boxster
<img class="pop" src="boxster.png" alt="Boxster">
</a>

<a href="#null">Carrera
<img class="pop" src="carrera.png" alt="Carrera">
</a>
</p>
```

4 Next in the body, insert a paragraph containing text
```
<p >
Porsche doesn't simply build sports cars.<br>Porsche is
more. Much more. And Porsche is different.
</p>
```

Hot tip

Specifiying a value of just "#" to a hyperlink's **href** attribute targets the top of that document.

...cont'd

5 Save the HTML document then create a style sheet that removes browser defaults and initially hides the images
`* { margin : 0 ; padding : 0 ; border : 0 ; }`
`img.pop`
`{ position : absolute ; top : 20px ; left : 190px ;`
`padding : 15px ; visibility : hidden ; height : 0px ; }`

popup.css

6 Next add rules to size and position both paragraphs
`p { width : 150px ; float : left ; margin : 20px 0 0 20px ; }`

7 Now add rules to style the hyperlinks
`p#models a`
`{ display : block ; padding : 5px ; margin : 0 0 20px 0 ;`
`color : white ; background : blue ; text-decoration : none ; }`

`p#models a:hover { color : #FFF ; background : #F00 ; }`

`p#models a:hover  img.pop`
`{ border : 5px solid red ; background : #FFF ;`
`z-index : 10 ; visibility : visible ; height : auto ; }`

8 Save the style sheet then open the web page in your browser and place the cursor over any hyperlink to see its associated image appear above the text paragraph

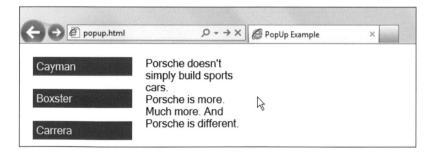

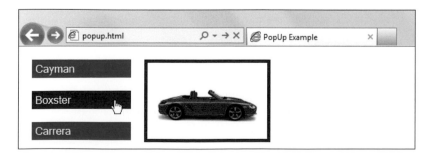

Don't forget

Notice that the foreground and background colors for the hyperlink's hover state are specified using hexadecimal shorthand values for red and white.

Summary

- The HTML5 **<a> </a>** anchor tags are used to enclose hyperlinks within a HTML document

- An **href** attribute can be included in an **<a>** anchor tag to specify the URL of a target resource for that hyperlink

- Each hyperlink is sensitive to hover, active, and visited states

- Hyperlinks can be accessed by a pointer, the tab key, or a designated key specified by the **<a>** tag's **accesskey** attribute

- An **id** attribute can be included in an element to create a fragment identifier that can become the target of a hyperlink

- When targeting a fragment the hyperlink's **href** attribute must specify the identifier name prefixed by a **#** hash character

- A hyperlink may target a resource via the **http:** protocol, or with other protocols such as **javascript:** and **mailto:**

- Rollover effects are performed by the CSS **a:hover** psuedo-class to swap images in response to cursor position

- A single image can target multiple hyperlink resources by adding an image map to specify an area for each hyperlink

- The **<map> </map>** tags enclose **<area>** elements, to define the areas of an image map, and a **name** attribute must be included in the **<map>** tag to specify a name for that map

- To use an image map the **<img>** tag must include a **usemap** attribute specifying the map's name prefixed by a **#** hash character

- Each **<area>** tag must include **shape**, **coords**, **href**, and **alt** attributes and the shape may be a value of **rect**, **circle**, or **poly**

- Hyperlinks can be used without resource targets to perform CSS effects by assigning a **#null** value to the **<a>** tag's **href** attribute

- Popup effects can be performed by the CSS **a:hover** psuedo-class to reveal hidden content in response to cursor position

5

Arranging content sections

This chapter demonstrates how to group content into sections within the body of an HTML5 document.

Proclaiming headings

HTML5 heading elements are created using **<h1>**, **<h2>**, **<h3>**, **<h4>**, **<h5>**, and **<h6>** tags. These are ranked in importance by their numeric value – where **<h1>** has the greatest importance, and **<h6>** has the least importance. Each heading requires a matching closing tag and should only contain heading text. Typically the heading's font size and weight will reflect its importance, but headings also serve other purposes.

Heading elements should be used to implicitly convey the document structure by correctly sequencing them – so **<h2>** elements below a **<h1>** element, **<h3>** elements below a **<h2>** element, and so on. This structure helps readers quickly skim through a document by navigating its headings.

Search engine spiders may promote documents that have correctly sequenced headings as they can use the headings in their index. They assume headings are likely to describe their content so it is especially useful to include meta keywords from the document's head section in the document's headings.

The **<h1>** element is by far the most important heading and should ideally appear only once to proclaim the document heading. Often this can be a succinct version of the document title. Below that a number of **<h2>** headings can proclaim section headings for long documents. Each section might contain individual article headings within **<h3>** elements, followed by paragraph **<p>** elements containing the actual article content.

heading.html

1 Start with the HTML5 document type declaration
<!DOCTYPE HTML>

2 Add a root element containing head and body sections
<html lang="en">
<head>
<meta charset="UTF-8"><title>Heading Example</title>
</head>
<body> <!-- Content to go here --> </body>
</html>

3 Within the body section, insert a main document heading
<h1>Document Heading</h1>

...cont'd

4 Next within the body section, insert a section heading
`<h2>Section Heading</h2>`

5 Now within the body section, insert some article headings
followed by paragraphs containing the article content
`<h3>Article Heading</h3> <p>Article content...</p>`
`<h3>Article Heading</h3> <p>Article content...</p>`

6 Finally add another section with two more articles
`<h2>Section Heading</h2>`
`<h3>Article Heading</h3> <p>Article content...</p>`
`<h3>Article Heading</h3> <p>Article content...</p>`

7 Save the HTML document then open it in your web
browser to see the headings and document structure

Beware

Never use heading elements for their font properties as these can be overridden by style sheet rules – always consider headings to represent structure.

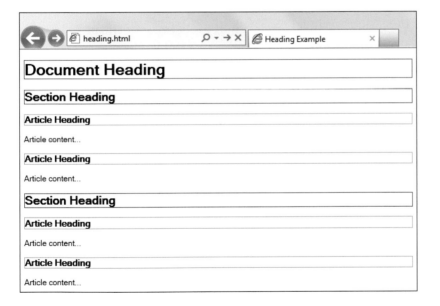

The document structure created by the sequenced headings is known as the document "outline". Properly constructed outlines allow a part of the page, such as a single article, to be easily syndicated into another site. The outline for the document above is illustrated alongside.

1. Document Heading
   1. Section Heading
      1. Article Heading
      2. Article Heading
   2. Section Heading
      1. Article Heading
      2. Article Heading

Hot tip

All screenshots throughout this chapter have added (unlisted) colored border styles to more clearly illustrate the page area occupied by the elements described.

Grouping headings

Headings sometimes have a sub-heading or tagline. For example, a document heading could be marked up like this:

```
<h1>American Airlines</h1>
<h2>Doing What We Do Best</h2>
```

Unfortunately this requires all subsequent headings to be **<h3>** down to **<h6>** – to maintain a correctly sequenced outline. Fortunately HTML5 provides a solution with the **<hgroup> </hgroup>** tags. These can be used to enclose both the heading and sub-heading, so that the **<h2>** element is effectively removed from the document outline. Any **<hgroup>** element is only defined by the highest ranking **<h1>** to **<h6>** element it contains.

```
<hgroup>
<h1>American Airlines</h1>
<h2>Doing What We Do Best</h2>
</hgroup>
```

When this example is wrapped in a **<hgroup>** element subsequent headings may now be **<h2>** down to **<h6>** – to maintain a correctly sequenced outline.

Complete headers may be enclosed in **<header> </header>** tags to include a single heading, or **<hgroup>** element, along with other introductory items – such as a logo or a section's table of contents. Typically a **<header>** element will contain the document heading at the start of a page, but may also be used at the start of sections within a page to contain associated introductory items.

hgroup.html

1 Start with the HTML5 document type declaration
```
<!DOCTYPE HTML>
```

2 Add a root element containing head and body sections
```
<html lang="en">
<head>
<meta charset="UTF-8">
<title>Heading Groups Example</title>
</head>
<body>  <!-- Content to go here --> </body>
</html>
```

3 Within the body section, insert a main document heading
```
<hgroup>
<h1>HTML5</h1><h2>Building better websites</h2>
</hgroup>
```

...cont'd

4 Next within the body section, insert a section and article
```
<h2>Section Heading</h2>
<h3>Article Heading</h3> <p> Article Content...</p>
```

5 Now within the body section, insert a second section with a single article
```
<hgroup>
<h1>CSS</h1> <h2>Cascading Style Sheets</h2>
</hgroup>
<h3>Article Heading</h3> <p>Article content...</p>
```

Hot tip

The **<header>** element is not required to simply enclose headings – it is only needed to enclose additional items.

6 Finally insert a logo into the main document heading
```
<header>
<img src="logo.png" alt="Logo">
<hgroup>
<h1>HTML5</h1><h2>Building better websites</h2>
</hgroup>
</header>
```

7 Save the HTML document then open it in your web browser to see the grouped headings and document header

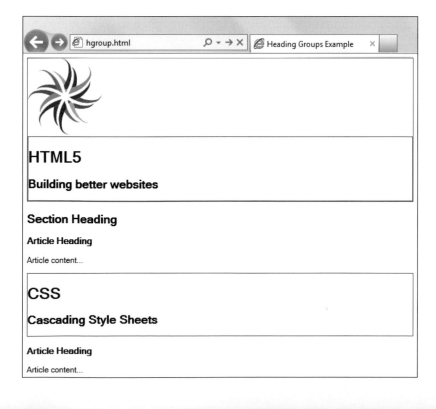

Don't forget

The **<hgroup>** elements here are only defined by their **<h1>** elements – their enclosed **<h2>** elements do not appear in the document outline.

```
1. HTML5
   1. Section Heading
      1. Article Heading
2. CSS
   1. Article Heading
```

Providing navigation

Groups of hyperlinks on a HTML5 web page, which enable the user to navigate around the page or website, should be enclosed between **<nav>** **</nav>** tags. This may typically be a horizontal menu in the document header, or a vertical menu down the edge of the page. Note that the **<nav>** element is simply a wrapper around the menu – it does not replace any structural elements.

nav.html

1 Start with the HTML5 document type declaration
```
<!DOCTYPE HTML>
```

2 Add a root element containing head and body sections, with a link element pointing to a style sheet
```
<html lang="en">
<head>
<meta charset="UTF-8">
<title>Navigation Example</title>
<link rel="stylesheet" href="nav.css">
</head>
<body>  <!-- Content to go here --> </body>
</html>
```

3 Within the body, insert a header containing a logo, document heading, and horizontal page navigation menu
```
<header>
<img id="logo" src="logo-sm.png" alt="Logo">
<h1>Building better websites</h1>
<nav id="horizontal">
<p>
<a href="#html">Markup</a> |
<a href="#js">Scripting</a> |
<a href="#css">Style Sheets</a> </p>
</nav>
</header>
```

Not every group of hyperlinks is eligible to be contained in a **<nav>** element – only those that provide page-wide or site-wide navigation.

4 Next in the body, insert a vertical site navigation menu
```
<nav id="vertical" >
<p>Further Reading<br>In Easy Steps:
<br><br> <a href="js.html">JavaScript</a>
<br><br> <a href="css.html">CSS</a> </p>
</nav>
```

5 Now add regular content then save the HTML document
```
<h2 id="html">HTML5</h2> <p>All about markup...</p>
<h2 id="js">JavaScript</h2><p>All about scripting...</p>
<h2 id="css" >CSS</h2> <p>All about stylesheets...</p>
```

6 Create a style sheet to position the logo image and
navigation menus

```
#logo   { float : left ; }
#horizontal      { padding-left : 100px ; display : block ; }
#vertical { float : left ; padding : 0px 30px 130px 30px ; }
```

nav.css

7 Save the HTML document and style sheet, then open the
web page in your browser and try out the navigation links

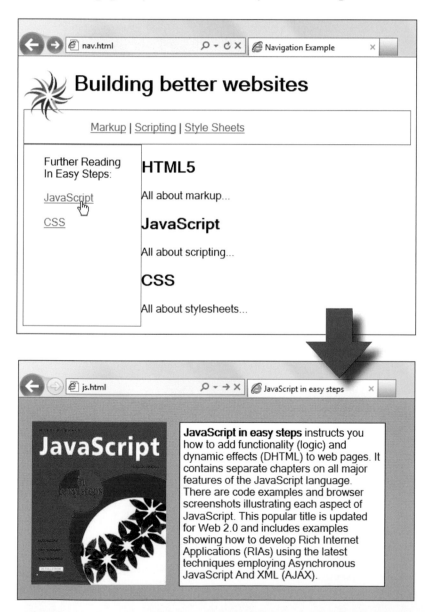

Hot tip

It is popular to create
vertical navigation menus
as unordered lists – see
ahead on page 98.

Writing articles

In HTML5 all content within the **<body>** element is considered to be part of a "section". Within the main section, defined by the **<body>** element, section limits are defined implicitly by correctly sequenced headings in the document outline. Section limits may also be defined explicitly by placing content within the **<header>**, **<nav>**, **<section>** and **<article>** elements, plus the **<aside>**, and **<footer>** elements demonstrated over the next few pages.

General content within the document body, which is not part of a special content element such as **<nav>**, can be arranged in sections between **<section> </section>** tags. Each section will typically begin with its own heading element followed by articles.

Each article should be enclosed between **<article> </article>** tags and will typically begin with its own heading element followed by one or more paragraphs.

In understanding the **<section>** and **<article>** elements it helps to consider the way a newspaper contains various sections – news, sport, real estate, and so on. Each section contains various articles.

1 Start with the HTML5 document type declaration
```
<!DOCTYPE HTML>
```

2 Add a root element containing head and body sections
```
<html lang="en">
<head>
<meta charset="UTF-8">
<title>Section Example</title>
</head>
<body>  <!-- Content to go here --> </body>
</html>
```

3 Within the body, insert a main document heading
```
<h1>Newspaper</h1>
```

4 Next in the body, insert two section elements
```
<section>
<!-- Articles to go here -->
</section>

<section>
<!-- Articles to go here -->
</section>
```

Hot tip

Remember that an **<article>** contains a stand-alone composition but a **<section>** is just a grouping element.

section.html

...cont'd

5 Within the first section element, insert a section heading
`<h2>News Section</h2>`

6 Now insert a section heading in the second section element
`<h2>Sport Section</h2>`

7 After the heading in each section, add two articles that each contain an article heading and a single paragraph
```
<article>
<h3>Article #1</h3>
<p>Article content...</p>
</article>

<article>
<h3>Article #2</h3>
<p>Article content...</p>
</article>
```

8 Save the HTML document then open it in your browser to see the article content displayed in sections

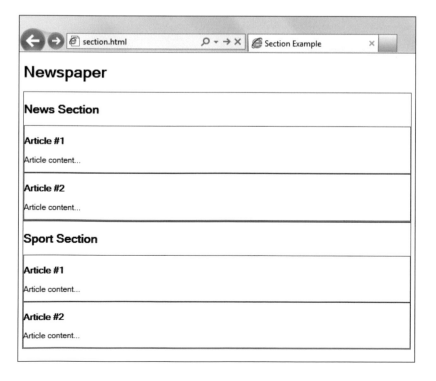

Don't forget

A lengthy `<article>` could even contain nested `<section>` elements, each containing nested `<article>` elements.

Don't forget

The document, section, and article headings appear correctly nested in the document outline.

1. <u>Newspaper</u>
   1. <u>News Section</u>
      1. <u>Article #1</u>
      2. <u>Article #2</u>
   2. <u>Sport Section</u>
      1. <u>Article #1</u>
      2. <u>Article #2</u>

Standing aside

HTML5 usefully provides **<aside> </aside>** tags that can be nested within an **<article>** element in order to incorporate content that is somewhat related to the main content of that article. These allow for supplemental, yet separate, content to be included – typically displayed as a sidebar or footnote.

Content within an **<aside>** element should be stand-alone information that is related to the article, such as pull-quotes extracted from an affiliated article, a glossary of terms used within the article, or even hyperlinks to pages providing further reading associated with the article.

Alternatively the **<aside>** element can be used alone, without an **<article>** element, to contain secondary content that is related to the entire page, such as related advertising or a blogroll.

aside.html

1 Start with the HTML5 document type declaration
<!DOCTYPE HTML>

2 Add a root element containing head and body sections, with a link element pointing to a style sheet
<html lang="en">
<head>
<meta charset="UTF-8">
<title>Aside Example</title>
<link rel="stylesheet" href="aside.css">
</head>
<body> <!-- Content to go here --> </body>
</html>

Hot tip

Avoid using the **<aside>** element to contain unrelated advertising.

3 Within the body, insert a main document heading
<h1>Famous Quotes</h1>

4 Next within the body, insert an article containing a heading, a paragraph, and an aside element
<article>
<h2>Cynicism</h2>
**<p> <q>A cynic is a man who knows the price of everything
but the value of nothing.</q>
**
<cite>Oscar Wilde</cite>
</p>
**<aside>Oscar Wilde (1854 – 1900)
**
was an Irish writer and poet.</aside>
</article>

...cont'd

5 Now within the body, insert a second article containing a heading, a paragraph, and an aside element

```
<article>
<h2>Happiness</h2>
<p><q>The secret of happiness is not in doing what one
likes, but in liking what one has to do.</q> <br>
<cite>James M. Barrie</cite>
</p>
<aside>James M. Barrie (1860 - 1937) was a Scottish
author and dramatist.</aside>
</article>
```

6 Insert an attribute into the opening tag of the first article element so it can be selected for sidebar styling

```
<article class="sidebar">
```

7 Create a style sheet to control the position of the paragraph and aside element in the first article

```
article.sidebar > p,aside
{ display : table-cell ; padding-right: 20px ; }
```

aside.css

8 Save the HTML document and the style sheet, then open the web page in your browser to see how the asides appear

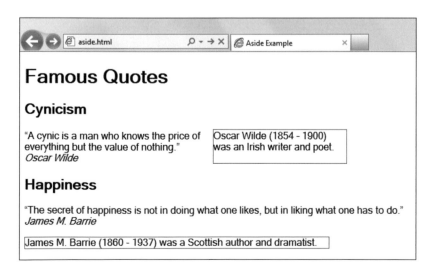

Beware

Do not use the **<aside>** element to contain navigation hyperlinks – those should always be contained inside a **<nav>** element.

Footing the page

Just as each HTML5 document may contain multiple headings, for the document, sections, and articles, they may also contain multiple footers for the document, sections, and articles. The content of each footer is contained between **<footer>** **</footer>** tags and provides information about that part of the document.

Typically a **<footer>** element might contain the author's name, the author's contact details within an **<address>** element, or copyright and legal disclaimers within a **<small>** element.

Like a **<header>** element, a **<footer>** element can also contain hyperlinks for page and site navigation within a nested **<nav>** element. Hyperlinks to related documents, however, are better placed in an **<aside>** element within the section or aticle.

footer.html

Don't forget

The HTML5 **<aside>** and **<nav>** elements may also each contain a **<footer>** element.

90

1 Start with the HTML5 document type declaration
<!DOCTYPE HTML>

2 Add a root element containing head and body sections, with a link element pointing to a style sheet
<html lang="en">
<head>
<meta charset="UTF-8">
<title>Footer Example</title>
<link rel="stylesheet" href="footer.css">
</head>
<body> <!-- Content to go here --> </body>
</html>

3 Within the body, insert a main document heading
<h1 id="top">Interesting Articles</h1>

4 Next within the body, just before its closing tag, insert a document footer containing page navigation hyperlinks
<footer id="page">
<nav>
<a href="#art-1">Sally's Article</a> -
<a href="#art-2">Terry's Article</a> -
<a href="#top">Top of Page</a>
</nav>
</footer>

5 Next within the document footer, insert copyright details
<small>Copyright © Example Corporation</small>

...cont'd

6 Now within the body, between the document heading and document footer, insert two articles that each contain an article heading, a paragraph, and an article footer

```
<article>
<h2 id="art-1">Sally's Article</h2>
<p>Article content...</p>
<footer>
<address>sally@example.com</address>
</footer>
</article>

<article>
<h2 id="art-2">Terry's Article</h2>
<p>Article content...</p>
<footer>
<address>terry@example.com</address>
</footer>
</article>
```

7 Create a style sheet to control the position of the page footer contents

```
footer#page { margin-top : 20px ; }
```

footer.css

8 Save the HTML document and the style sheet, then open the web page in your browser to see how the footers appear

Hot tip

<section> elements are not required in short documents like this one – unless you particularly want to add section headings and footers.

Denying anonymity

The dividing **<div>** **</div>** tags, which were used widely in earlier versions of HTML, continue to be supported in HTML5 for backward-compatibility – but the **<div>** element should only now be used as a last resort, when no other element is suitable. Unlike other meaningful elements such as **<header>**, **<section>**, **<article>**, **<nav>** and **<footer>**, the meaningless **<div>** element is anonymous. For example, a smart browser might have a shortcut key to jump to the page's navigation section. This section is easily identifiable when contained in a meaningful **<nav>** element, but not so when contained in a meaningless **<div>** element.

The **<div>** element remains useful for styling purposes, as do the similarly anonymous **<span>** **</span>** tags. Although the **<div>** and **<span>** elements are meaningless alone, they can include an identifying attribute to wrap content that is to be styled alike.

Documents that use the **<div>** element for structural, rather than stylistic, purposes should be edited to use meaningful elements instead. For example, given the body section elements below:

```
<div class="header">
<h1>Web Languages</h1>
</div>

<div class="nav">
<h2>Menu</h2>
<p><a href="js.html">JavaScript</a></p>
<p><a href="css.html">Cascading Style Sheets</a></p>
</div>

<div class="section">
<h2>HyperText <span>Markup</span> Language</h2>
<p>All about HTML...</p>

<h2>eXtensible <span>Markup</span> Language</h2>
<p>All about XML...</p>
</div>

<div class="footer">
<p><small>Copyright &copy; Example Corporation</small></p>
</div>
```

It should hopefully be obvious, especially given these class attribute values, that each anonymous **<div>** element can be easily replaced by more meaningful **<header>**, **<nav>**, **<section>**, **<article>**, and **<footer>** elements.

division.html
(body section)

...cont'd

1 Replace the "header" class **<div>** with a **<header>** element
<header> <h1>Web Languages</h1> </header>

2 Replace the "nav" class **<div>** with a **<nav>** element
<nav> <h2>Menu</h2>
<p><a href="js.html">JavaScript</a></p>
<p><a href="css.html">Cascading Style Sheets</a></p>
</nav>

3 Replace the "section" class **<div>** with **<section>** and
<article> elements
<section>
<article>
<h2>HyperText <span>Markup</span> Language</h2>
<p>All about HTML...</p> </article>
<article>
<h2>eXtensible <span>Markup</span> Language</h2>
<p>All about XML...</p> </article>
</section>

4 Replace the "footer" class **<div>** with a **<footer>** element
<footer> <p>
<small>Copyright © Example Corporation</small>
</p> </footer>

5 Save the document then open it in your browser to see it
appears the same – but it now has meaningful structure

Don't forget

Also amend any
associated style sheet to
select the new elements.

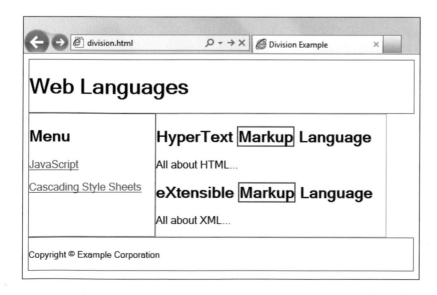

Positioning content

Although the use of the anonymous **<div>** element is generally best avoided it is useful to control the size and position of the entire page. A page designed for the popular resolution of 1024x768 pixels will overflow when viewed at a resolution of 640x480 so, as a compromise, many web page authors design pages for a resolution of 800x600. Some like to leave the page fixed horizontally at the default left position but many prefer to center the page for larger resolutions. Centering the page is achieved using a **<div>** element as a "wrapper" around all body content and applying a style rule to set its **margin** property to **auto**.

Additionally, many web page authors use the special * universal CSS selector to set the initial **padding, margin,** and **border** properties to zero – removing the default browser values. This means that the **<div>** wrapper element gets positioned at the very top of the browser window.

The areas at each side of the centered wrapper reveal the background of the **<body>** element, which can be set to match the page background, or set to a different color for contrast, or styled with a background image tile.

Any content box on the page can also be centered within its containing element by setting its **margin** property to **auto**. The browser calculates the distance to the left and right of that content box, up to the boundaries of its containing element, then divides the total in half to compute the value of each side margin. For example, when applying a **margin:auto** rule to a **<p>** paragraph content box that is 500 pixels wide, contained within an outer wrapper element that is 800 pixels wide, the browser divides the total difference of 300 pixels in half then applies margins to each side of the paragraph of 150 pixels in width.

Notice that **margin:auto** does not center vertically but merely sets the top and bottom margins to zero – so there are no margin areas above or below the horizontally centered content box.

It is important to recognize that the **margin:auto** rule only centers the content box, but not the content within. In order to center the inner content a **text-align:center** rule must be applied to the element. The browser then calculates the distance to the left and right of the inline phrasing box, divides the total in half, then applies margins of that width to each side of the phrasing box.

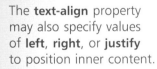

1 Insert a wrapper within the body section of a document
```
<div id="wrapper">
<!-- Content to go here -->
</div>
```

position.html

2 In the wrapper, insert an article containing a nested article
```
<article>
<h1>Default Heading Position</h1>
<p class="sized">Default Block Position</p>
  <article>
  <h1 class="center-text">Centered Heading</h1>
  <p class="sized center">Centered Block</p>
  <p class="sized center center-text">
        Centered Block<br>and<br>Centered Text</p>
  </article>
</article>
```

3 Create a style sheet to remove browser default styles,
center some content boxes, and center some inner text
```
* { padding : 0 ; margin : 0 ; border : 0 ; }

body    { background : #A9A9A9 ;          }

div#wrapper
{ margin : auto ; background : white ;
        width : 800px ; height : 1000px ; }

.sized          { width : 40% ;   }
.center         { margin : auto ; }
.center-text    { text-align : center ;  }
```

position.css

4 Save the HTML document and style sheet then open the
web page in your browser to see the rules position content

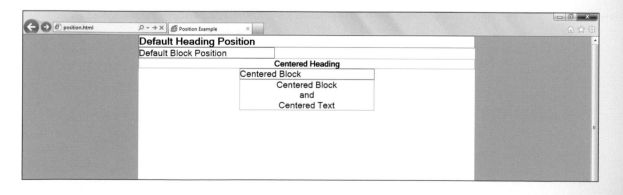

Summary

- Heading elements **<h1>**, **<h2>**, **<h3>**, **<h4>**, **<h5>**, and **<h6>** are ranked in order of importance from **<h1>** down to **<h6>**

- Correctly sequenced heading elements implicitly convey the document structure, to create the document outline

- Any **<hgroup>** element is only defined in the document outline by the highest ranking **<h1>** to **<h6>** element it contains

- Complete headers, including a logo and a heading or **<hgroup>** element, can be enclosed in a **<header>** element

- Groups of hyperlinks providing page or site navigation should be enclosed within a **<nav>** element

- A **<nav>** element is just a wrapper around a menu, typically displayed horizontally in the header or vertically in a sidebar

- Section limits are explicitly defined in a document outline when content is placed within **<header>**, **<nav>**, **<section>**, **<article>**, **<aside>**, and **<footer>** elements

- Each document **<section>** element will typically begin with a section heading, followed by one or more articles

- Each document **<article>** element will typically begin with an article heading, followed by one or more paragraphs

- Stand-alone information related to an article can be enclosed within an **<aside>** element nested in an **<article>** element

- Typically a **<footer>** element might contain contact details in an **<address>** element or legal details in a **<small>** element

- The anonymous **<div>** and **<span>** elements are best avoided for structural purposes, but are useful for styling purposes

- A **<div>** element can be used as a wrapper around all body content to control the size and position of the page

- The **margin:auto** style rule centers content boxes, whereas the **text-align:center** rule centers text within content boxes

6

Writing lists and tables

This chapter demonstrates how to create lists and tables in the body section of an HTML5 document.

Creating unordered lists

Unordered lists, where the sequence of list items is not important, typically place a bullet-point before each item to differentiate list items from regular text.

In HTML5 unordered lists are created with **<ul> </ul>** tags, which provide a container for list items. Each list item can be created using **<li> </li>** tags to enclose the item, or optionally just using **<li>** to precede the item – either form of **<li>** element validates as correct HTML. An unordered list **<ul>** element can contain numerous list item **<li>** elements.

The bullet point that differentiates unordered list items from regular text may be one of these three marker types:

- **Disc** – a filled circular bullet-point (the default style)

- **Circle** – an unfilled circular bullet-point

- **Square** – a filled square bullet-point

A style rule can specify any one of the above values to the unordered list's **list-style-type** property, or a **none** value can be specified to that property to suppress bullet-points.

Each HTML list also has a **list-style-image** property that can specify the URL of an image to be used as the list's bullet-point. This will appear in place of any of the marker type bullet-points. Where the web browser cannot use the specified image the marker specified to its **list-style-type** property will be used, or when no marker has been specified the default will be used.

ulist.html

1 Start with the HTML5 document type declaration
<!DOCTYPE HTML>

2 Add a root element containing head and body sections, with a link element pointing to a style sheet
<html lang="en">
<head>
<meta charset="UTF-8">
<title>Unordered List Example</title>
<link rel="stylesheet" href="ulist.css">
</head>
<body>   <!-- Content to go here --> </body>
</html>

...cont'd

3 Within the body section, insert four copies of this complete unordered list, with no specified class name
```
<ul class="">
<li>JavaScript</li>
<li>Cascading Style Sheets</li>
<li>C Programming</li>
</ul>
```

Hot tip

Note that in CSS terms the lists are written in a content box with their bullet-points drawn in its left padding area.

4 Now edit each list in turn to provide a class name
```
<ul class=" disc-bullets">
<ul class=" circle-bullets">
<ul class=" square-bullets">
<ul class=" image-bullets">
```

5 Next make the final list into a site navigation menu, by enclosing it within a **<nav>** element and making each list item into a hyperlink
```
<nav> <ul class=" image-bullets">
<li><a href="script.html">JavaScript</a></li>
<li><a href="style.html">Cascading Style Sheets</a></li>
<li><a href="program.html">C Programming</a></li>
</ul> </nav>
```

6 Create a style sheet to position each list and to specify their individual bullet-point styles
```
ul.disc-bullets    { list-style-type : disc ; float : left ; }
ul.circle-bullets   { list-style-type : circle ; float : left ; }
ul.square-bullets { list-style-type : square ; float : left ; }
ul.image-bullets
{ list-style-image : url( go.png ) ; clear : both ; }
```

ulist.css

7 Save the HTML document and style sheet then open the web page in your browser to see the list bullet points

go.png 21px x 21px

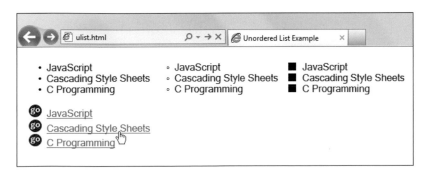

Creating ordered lists

Ordered lists, where the sequence of list items is important, number each item to differentiate list items from regular text.

In HTML5 ordered lists are created with **<ol> </ol>** tags, which provide a container for list items. As with unordered lists each list item can be created using **<li> </li>** tags to enclose the item, or optionally just using **<li>** to precede the item – either form of **<li>** element validates as correct HTML. An ordered list **<ol>** element can contain numerous list item **<li>** elements.

The automatic numbering that differentiates ordered list items from regular text may be one of these six numbering types:

- **Decimal** – traditional numerals (the default style)

- **Roman** – classical numerals

- **Latin** – traditional alphabetical lettering

- **Greek** – classical alphabetical lettering

- **Georgian** – traditional Georgian numbering

- **Armenian** – traditional Armenian numbering

A style rule can specify any of the above numbering types to the list's **list-style-type** property with the following values:

Type:	Value:
Decimal	**decimal** or **decimal-leading-zero**
Roman	**lower-roman** or **upper-roman**
Latin	**lower-latin** or **upper-latin** **lower-alpha** or **upper-alpha**
Greek	**lower-greek**
Georgian	**georgian**
Armenian	**armenian**

Additionally a **none** value can be specified to suppress numbering. List item numbering will normally begin at one but a different start point can be specified to a **start** attribute in the **<ol>** tag.

...cont'd

1 Start with the HTML5 document type declaration
```
<!DOCTYPE HTML>
```

olist.html

2 Add a root element containing head and body sections, with a link element pointing to a style sheet
```
<html lang="en">
<head>
<meta charset="UTF-8">
<title>Ordered List Example</title>
<link rel="stylesheet" href="olist.css">
</head>
<body>  <!-- Content to go here --> </body>
</html>
```

3 Within the body section, insert three ordered lists
```
<ol id="list-1">
<li>Cheetah<li>Pronghorn Antelope<li>Blue Wildebeest</li>
</ol>
<ol id="list-2">
<li>Lion<li>Springbok<li>Brown Hare</li>
</ol>
<ol id="list-3">
<li>Nile<li>Amazon<li>Mississippi</li>
</ol>
```

4 Now edit the second list to begin numbering at four
```
<ol id="list-2" start="4">
```

5 Create a style sheet to position the lists and to specify how the items should be numbered
```
ol { display : table-cell ; }
ol#list-2 { padding-right : 20px ; }
ol#list-3 { list-style-type : upper-roman ;
padding-left : 50px ; border-left : 3px dashed black ; }
```

olist.css

6 Save the HTML document and style sheet then open the web page in your browser to see the list numbering

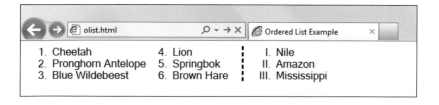

Creating definition lists

A definition list is a unique type of list in which each list item has two parts – the first part being a term, and the second part being a description of the term in the first part. This is referred to as a name/value pair. For example, a name/value pair for the the term "sun" could be "sun/the star at the center of our solar system".

In HTML5 definition lists are created with **<dl> </dl>** tags, which provide a container for list items. Each list item term is contained between **<dt> </dt>** definition term tags, and each list item description is contained between **<dd> </dd>** definition description tags. Optionally the **</dt>** and **</dd>** closing tags may be omitted – either form of **<dt>** and **<dd>** element is valid.

Each list item in a definition list can contain multiple **<dt>** definition term elements and multiple **<dd>** definition description elements – to allow a single term to have multiple descriptions, or multiple terms to have a single description. Typically browsers display the definition descriptions inset from their terms.

Definition lists are also useful to contain a series of questions and related answers, or indeed any other groups of name/value data.

dlist.html

1 Start with the HTML5 document type declaration
<!DOCTYPE HTML>

2 Add a root element containing head and body sections, with a link element pointing to a style sheet
```
<html lang="en">
<head>
<meta charset="UTF-8">
<title>Definition List Example</title>
<link rel="stylesheet" href="dlist.css">
</head>
<body>  <!-- Content to go here --> </body>
</html>
```

3 Within the body section, insert a definition list containing two question and answer name/value pairs
```
<dl>
  <dt>What is HTML5?</dt>
  <dd>The latest HyperText Markup Language</dd>

  <dt>When can I use it?</dt>
  <dd>Right now.</dd>
</dl>
```

4 Next in the body section insert a second definition list containing two list items that each have multiple descriptions – describing the use, pronunciation, and meaning of their term

```
<dl>
<dt><dfn>Homonym</dfn></dt>
<dd class="grammar">noun</dd>
<dd class="spoken">[hom-uh-nim]</dd>
<dd>a word the same as another in sound and spelling
but different in meaning</dd>

<dt><dfn>Mouse</dfn></dt>
<dd class="grammar">noun</dd>
<dd class="spoken">[mous]</dd>
<dd>a small animal of various rodent families</dd>
<dd>a palm-sized button-operated device used to move a
computer cursor</dd>
<dd>a quiet, timid person</dd>
</dl>
```

5 Create a style sheet to color the question and definition terms in the lists and to color some specific descriptions

```
dt { color : blue ; }
dfn { color : red ; font-size : 20pt ; }
dd.grammar { color : green ; }
dd.spoken { color : blue ; }
```

6 Save the HTML document and style sheet then open the web page in your browser to see the name/value pairs

Don't forget

The **<dt>** element alone does not indicate its content is a term being defined – a nested **<dfn>** element must be used for that purpose.

dlist.css

103

Beware

Do not use a definition list to mark up dialog – use paragraphs to mark up each piece of dialog instead.

dlist.html   Definition List Example

What is HTML5?
   The latest HyperText Markup Language
When can I use it?
   Right now.

Homonym
   noun
   [hom-uh-nim]
   a word the same as another in sound and spelling but different in meaning
Mouse
   noun
   [mous]
   a small animal of various rodent families
   a palm-sized button-operated device used to move a computer cursor
   a quiet, timid person

Producing a simple table

Data is often best presented in tabular form, arranged in rows and columns to logically group related items, so it is easily understood.

In HTML5 tables are created with **<table> </table>** tags, which provide a container for table rows. Each table row is created with **<tr> </tr>** tags, which provide a container for a line of table data cells. Each table data cell is created with **<td> </td>** tags, which enclose the actual data to be presented. Optionally the **</td>** and **</tr>** closing tags may be omitted – either form of **<td>** and **<tr>** element is valid.

A **<table>** element will typically contain numerous **<tr>** elements to create a table displaying multiple rows of data. Similarly each **<tr>** element will typically contain numerous **<td>** elements to create a table of multiple columns of data. It is important to note, however, that each **<tr>** row in the table must contain the exact same number of **<td>** cells – so for example if the first **<tr>** row contains five **<td>** cells, all **<tr>** rows must contain five **<td>** cells.

table.html

1 Start with the HTML5 document type declaration
```
<!DOCTYPE HTML>
```

2 Add a root element containing head and body sections, with a link element pointing to a style sheet
```
<html lang="en">
<head>
<meta charset="UTF-8">
<title>Table Example</title>
<link rel="stylesheet" href="table.css">
</head>
<body> <!-- Content to go here --> </body>
</html>
```

3 Within the body section, insert a table element that includes an identity for styling purposes
```
<table id="data">
<!-- Table rows to go here -->
</table>
```

4 Now within the table element, insert three rows that each contain three table data cells
```
<tr> <td>Cell 1.1 <td>Cell 1.2 <td>Cell 1.3 </tr>
<tr> <td>Cell 2.1 <td>Cell 2.2 <td>Cell 2.3 </tr>
<tr> <td>Cell 3.1 <td>Cell 3.2 <td>Cell 3.3 </tr>
```

5 Create a style sheet to set the table width and font, and also to add borders to the table, its cells, and its headings (added later below)
table#data { width : 580px ; font-family : sans-serif ; border : 5px solid black ; }
table#data td,th { border : 1px solid black ; }

table.css

6 Save the HTML document and style sheet then open the web page to see this simple table

Cell 1.1	Cell 1.2	Cell 1.3
Cell 2.1	Cell 2.2	Cell 2.3
Cell 3.1	Cell 3.2	Cell 3.3

table.html — Table Example

A table title can be specified between **<caption> </caption>** tags, which may only appear immediately after the **<table>** tag. Row and column headings can also be added between **<th> </th>** tags. The number of **<th>** headings must exactly match the number of rows and columns, and the **</th>** closing tag is also optional.

7 Immediately following the opening table tag, insert a caption title and a new row of four column headings
<caption>A Simple Table</caption>
<tr><th><th>Column 1<th>Column 2<th>Column 3</tr>

Don't forget

8 Finally insert a row heading at the start of each following row then save the HTML document to view the additions
<tr><th>Row 1<td>Cell 1.1<td>Cell 1.2<td>Cell 1.3</tr>
<tr><th>Row 2<td>Cell 2.1<td>Cell 2.2<td>Cell 2.3</tr>
<tr><th>Row 3<td>Cell 3.1<td>Cell 3.2<td>Cell 3.3</tr>

Subsequent examples in this chapter build upon this simple table example as more table features are introduced.

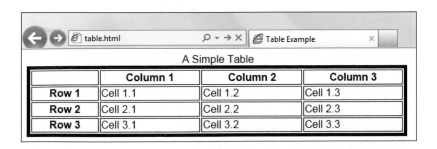

table.html — Table Example

A Simple Table

	Column 1	Column 2	Column 3
Row 1	Cell 1.1	Cell 1.2	Cell 1.3
Row 2	Cell 2.1	Cell 2.2	Cell 2.3
Row 3	Cell 3.1	Cell 3.2	Cell 3.3

Spanning cells over rows

An individual table cell can be combined with others vertically to span down over multiple rows of a table. The number of rows to be spanned is specified to a **rowspan** attribute in the spanning cell's **<td>** tag. Cells in the rows being spanned must then be removed to maintain the table symmetry.

rowspan.html

1 Make a copy of the **table.html** document, created in the previous example, and rename it "rowspan.html"

2 Change the document and table titles
<title>Row Spanning Example</title>
<caption>A Table Spanning Rows</caption>

3 In the table data element containing the text "Cell 1.1", insert an attribute in its opening tag and edit its content
<td rowspan="2">Cell 1.1+2.1</td>

4 Now delete the table data element containing the text "Cell 2.1" – as this cell is now spanned

table.css
(additions)

5 Save the HTML document then re-open the **table.css** style sheet and add rules to style cells spanning rows
table#data td[rowspan="2"] { background : yellow ; }
table#data td[rowspan="3"] { background : aqua ; }

6 Save the style sheet then open the web page in your browser to see the cell spanning two rows in Column 1

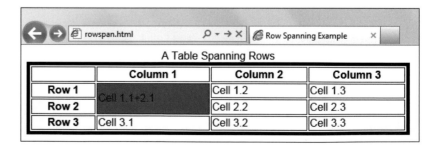

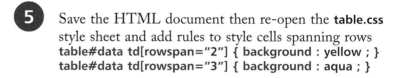

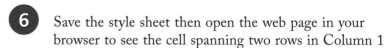

...cont'd

7 Re-open the HTML document then insert an attribute into the table data element containing the text "Cell 2.2" and edit its content
`<td rowspan="2">Cell 2.2+3.2</td>`

8 Now delete the table data element containing the text "Cell 3.2" – as this cell is now spanned

9 Save the amended HTML document then open it in your browser to see the cell spanning two rows in Column 2

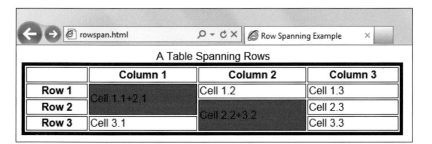

Hot tip

Insert tab spaces between all table data elements in the HTML code to align them so it's easier to configure the table layout.

10 Re-open the HTML document once more then insert an attribute into the table data element containing the text "Cell 1.3" and edit its content
`<td rowspan="3">Cell 1.3+2.3+3.3</td>`

11 Now delete the table data elements containing the text "Cell 2.3" and "Cell 3.3" – as these cells are now spanned

12 Save the amended HTML document then open it in your browser to see the cell spanning three rows in Column 3

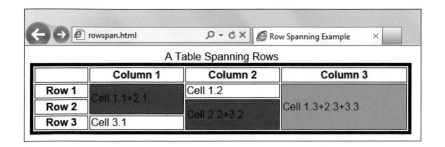

Don't forget

Notice that by default text in each cell is left-aligned and vertically centered in merged cells.

Spanning cells across columns

An individual table cell can be combined with others horizontally to span to the right across multiple columns of a table. The number of columns to be spanned is specified to a **colspan** attribute in the spanning cell's **<td>** tag. Cells in the columns being spanned must then be removed to maintain table symmetry.

colspan.html

1 Make a copy of the **table.html** document, created on pages 104-105, and rename it "colspan.html"

2 Change the document and table titles
<title>Column Spanning Example</title>
<caption>A Table Spanning Columns</caption>

3 In the table data element containing the text "Cell 1.1", insert an attribute in its opening tag and edit its content
<td colspan="2">Cell 1.1+1.2</td>

4 Now delete the table data element containing the text "Cell 1.2" – as this cell is now spanned

5 Save the HTML document then re-open the **table.css** style sheet and add rules to style cells spanning columns
table#data td[colspan="2"] { background : aqua ; }
table#data td[colspan="3"] { background : yellow ; }

table.css
(additions)

6 Save the style sheet then open the web page in your browser to see the cell spanning two columns on Row 1

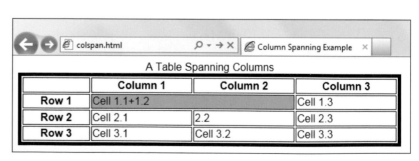

	colspan.html		Column Spanning Example
	A Table Spanning Columns		
	Column 1	Column 2	Column 3
Row 1	Cell 1.1+1.2		Cell 1.3
Row 2	Cell 2.1	2.2	Cell 2.3
Row 3	Cell 3.1	Cell 3.2	Cell 3.3

7 Re-open the HTML document then insert an attribute into the table data element containing the text "Cell 2.1" and edit its content
`<td colspan="3">Cell 2.1+2.2+2.3</td>`

8 Now delete the table data elements containing the text "Cell 2.2" and "Cell 2.3" – as these cells are now spanned

9 Save the amended HTML document then open it in your browser to see the cell spanning three columns on Row 2

Don't forget

Combined spans are rectangular – they cannot span an L-shape.

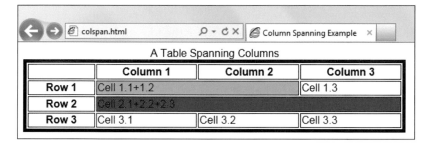

	Column 1	Column 2	Column 3
Row 1	Cell 1.1+1.2		Cell 1.3
Row 2	Cell 2.1+2.2+2.3		
Row 3	Cell 3.1	Cell 3.2	Cell 3.3

A Table Spanning Columns

109

10 Re-open the HTML document once more then insert another attribute into the table data element containing the text "Cell 2.1+2.2+2.3" and edit its content
`<td colspan="3" rowspan="2">`
`Cell 2.1+2.2+2.3+3.1+3.2+3.3</td>`

11 Now delete the table data elements containing the text "Cell 3.1". "Cell 3.2", and "Cell 3.3" – as these cells are now spanned

12 Save the amended HTML document then open it in your browser to see the cell span three columns and two rows

Hot tip

Column spanning and row spanning can be combined to create large rectangular blocks of cells extending over multiple columns and across multiple rows.

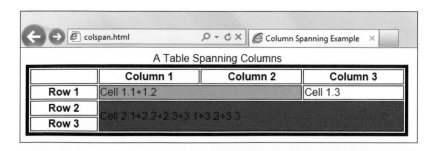

A Table Spanning Columns

	Column 1	Column 2	Column 3
Row 1	Cell 1.1+1.2		Cell 1.3
Row 2	Cell 2.1+2.2+2.3+3.1+3.2+3.3		
Row 3			

Adding a header and footer

Tables can be enhanced by the addition of special header and footer rows, above and below the regular table content, which provide additional table information.

In HTML5 table header information is contained between **<thead>** **</thead>** tags and table footer information is contained between **<tfoot>** **</tfoot>** tags. When a table has a **<thead>** and/or a **<tfoot>** element all regular table rows must be enclosed between **<tbody>** **</tbody>** tags.

In long tables rows can be grouped into separate table body sections using multiple **<tbody>** elements. When these are printed each paper page can repeat the table header and footer information.

It is important to note that both the **<thead>** and **<tfoot>** elements must appear before the first **<tbody>** element within the **<table>** element, but after the **<caption>** element if one is present.

enhance.html

1. Make a copy of the **table.html** document, created on pages 104-105, and rename it "enhance.html"

2. Change the document and table titles
   <title>Enhanced Table Example</title>
   <caption>An Enhanced Table</caption>

3. Immediately after the caption, insert a table header containing a single row that spans all four columns
   <thead>
   <tr><td colspan="4">Header Information</tr>
   </thead>

4. Immediately after the header, insert a table footer containing a single row that spans all four columns
   <tfoot>
   <tr><td colspan="4">Footer Information</tr>
   </tfoot>

5. After the footer, add a table body element to enclose all the regular existing table rows
   <tbody>
   <!-- Existing row elements go here -->
   </tbody>

6 After the table body element, insert a second table body element containing four more table rows

```
<tbody>
<tr><th colspan="4" class="next">Next section</tr>
<tr>
<th>Row 4<td>Cell 4.1<td>Cell 4.2<td>Cell 4.3</tr>
<tr>
<th>Row 5<td>Cell 5.1<td>Cell 5.2<td>Cell 5.3</tr>
<tr>
<th>Row 6<td>Cell 6.1<td>Cell 6.2<td>Cell 6.3</tr>
</tbody>
```

7 Save the HTML document then re-open the **table.css** style sheet and add rules to style the table header, the second table body heading, and the table footer

```
table#data thead { background : aqua ; }
table#data th.next { background : yellow ; }
table#data tfoot { background : lime ; }
```

table.css
(additions)

8 Save the style sheet then open the web page in your browser to see the enhanced table

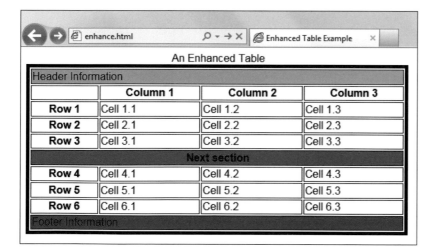

Don't forget

Table headers and footers should only contain information – all table data should appear in the table body.

Aligning cell content

Typically the default alignment of content in a **<td>** table data cell is horizontally left-aligned and vertically centered, whereas content in a **<th>** table heading cell is generally centered both horizontally and vertically. These defaults may be overridden by style rules, however, to align content horizontally and vertically.

A table cell's **text-align** property can specify values of **left**, **center**, or **right** to align horizontally, and its **vertical-align** property can specify values of **top**, **middle**, or **bottom** to align vertically.

Alignment rules may be specified for **<tr>**, **<tbody>**, **<thead>**, and **<tfoot>** elements to control the horizontal and vertical content position in groups of cells. All **<td>** and **<th>** elements they contain automatically inherit the specified alignment values.

align.html

1 Make a copy of the **table.html** document, created on pages 104-105, and rename it "align.html"

2 Change the document and table titles
<title>**Alignment Example**</title>
<caption>**A Table With Aligned Content**</caption>

3 Now edit each table row element to assign class names for styling content alignment
<tr class="**default**">
<th>**Row 1**<td>**Cell 1.1**<td>**Cell 1.2**<td>**Cell 1.3**</tr>
<tr class="**center**">
<th>**Row 2**<td>**Cell 2.1**<td>**Cell 2.2**<td>**Cell 2.3**</tr>
<tr class="**bottom right**">
<th>**Row 3**<td>**Cell 3.1**<td>**Cell 3.2**<td>**Cell 3.3**</tr>

table.css
(additions)

4 Save the HTML document then re-open the **table.css** style sheet and add rules to style cell content alignment, cell height, and background color
table#data tr.default td
{ height : 30px ; background : yellow ;}
table#data tr.center td
{ text-align : center ; height : 30px; background : aqua ; }
table#data tr.right td
{ text-align : right ; height : 30px ; background : lime ; }
table#data tr.bottom { vertical-align : bottom ; }

5 Save the style sheet then open the web page in your browser to compare the cell content alignment on each row

...cont'd

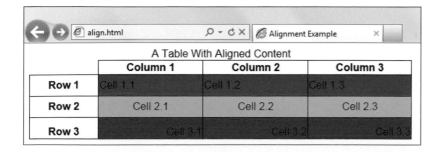

Table cells are automatically spaced apart at a fixed distance by default, but the cell spacing can be removed by a style rule specifying a **collapse** value to the table's **border-collapse** property. The outer table border can be explicitly suppressed by a style rule specifying a **none** value to the table's **border** property, and individual cell borders can be removed by a style rule specifying a value of **zero** to the cell's **border** property. For tables without outer borders it is particularly useful to remove the top left empty cell.

6 Edit the **align.html** document to assign class names for styling the table element and the top left empty table cell
```
<table id="data" class="no-border">
<tr><th class="cut-border">
<th>Column 1<th>Column 2<th>Column 3</tr>
```

7 Re-open the **table.css** style sheet again and add rules to remove the table and top left cell borders, and cell spacing
```
table#data.no-border
{ border-collapse : collapse ; border : none ; }
table#data tr th.cut-border { border : 0 ; }
```

8 Save the HTML document and style sheet once more then re-open the web page to see the borders removed

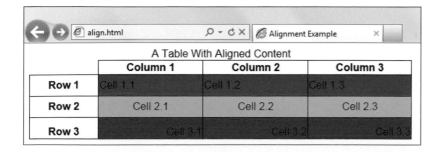

Don't forget

Notice that the final row aligns content to the bottom of each cell in both **<th>** and **<td>** elements as they inherit the rule applied to that row's **<tr>** element.

Hot tip

Cell and table borders can be removed or styled individually using their **border-top**, **border-right**, **border-bottom**, and **border-left** properties.

Grouping columns

Table columns that contain similar data can be virtually grouped together for styling purposes with **<colgroup> </colgroup>** tags. The opening **<colgroup>** tag can specify the number of columns to include in that group to a **span** attribute.

A **<table>** element can contain one or more **<colgroup>** elements to allow all the columns in a group to be styled alike, but have each group styled different to other groups for contrast. These should appear at the start of the **<table>** element, immediately after the **<caption>** element, if one is present, but before **<thead>**, **<tfoot>**, **<tbody>** elements and table content.

When the **<colgroup>** element includes a **span** attribute, to specify how many columns to include in that group, the closing **</colgroup>** tag is required but the element must remain empty – with nothing between the **<colgroup> </colgroup>** tags.

colgroup.html

1 Start with the HTML5 document type declaration
<!DOCTYPE HTML>

2 Add a root element containing head and body sections, with a link element pointing to a style sheet
<html lang="en">
<head>
<meta charset="UTF-8">
<title>Column Grouping Example</title>
<link rel="stylesheet" href="colgroup.css">
</head>
<body> <!-- Content to go here --> </body>
</html>

3 Within the body section, insert a table element that includes an identity for styling purposes
<table id="feb">
<!-- Table content to go here -->
</table>

4 Within the table element, first insert a table caption title
<caption>Monthly Calendar</caption>

5 Next within the table element, insert elements grouping columns – with specified class names for styling each group
<colgroup span="5" class="weekday"></colgroup>
<colgroup span="2" class="weekend"></colgroup>

6 Now within the table element, insert a table header and a table footer – each spanning seven columns

```
<thead>
<tr><th colspan="7">February 2021</tr>
</thead>

<tfoot>
<tr><th colspan="7">Birthday</tr>
</tfoot>
```

The table body in this example omits the optional **</td>** and **</tr>** closing tags to save page space, but including the **</tr>** tags more clearly denotes each row end.

7 Finally in the table element, insert a table body containing seven columns, with one cell given an identity for styling

```
<tbody>
<tr><td>Mon<td>Tue<td>Wed<td>Thu
<td>Fri<td>Sat<td>Sun<tr><td>1<td>2<td>3<td>4
<td>5<td>6<td>7<tr><td>8<td>9<td>10<td>11
<td>12<td>13<td>14<tr><td>15<td>16<td>17
<td>18<td>19<td>20<td id="birthday">21<tr>
<td>22<td>23<td>24<td>25<td>26<td>27<td>28
</tbody>
```

8 Create a style sheet to color the column groups, remove cell spacing, and highlight the header, footer, and one cell

```
table#feb colgroup.weekday { background : aqua ; }
table#feb colgroup.weekend { background : yellow ; }

table#feb { width : 580px ; border-collapse : collapse ; }
table#feb  thead,tfoot { background : white ; color : red ; }
table#feb tbody { text-align : center ; }
table#feb tbody tr td#birthday { border : 2px solid red ; }
```

colgroup.css

9 Save the HTML document and style sheet then open the web page in your browser to see how the column groups are clearly distinct from each other

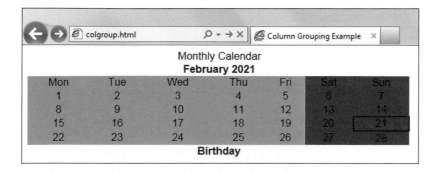

Setting column widths

Where a table simply has an overall width specified by a style rule the browser will by default calculate the width of each column according to its content – columns with broad content will be wider than columns with slender content. Greater control over column width can be achieved using **<col>** tags to represent individual columns so rules can specify their size and appearance.

A single **<col>** element can also represent multiple columns by including a **span** attribute to specify a number of columns. So a style rule specifying a column width will be applied to all the columns that **<col>** element represents.

Optionally **<col>** elements may be enclosed between **<colgroup>** **</colgroup>** tags to allow styling of both column groups and individual columns.

Don't forget

The **<col>** tag is a single tag – it does not have a matching closing tag.

column.html

1 Start with the HTML5 document type declaration
<!DOCTYPE HTML>

2 Add a root element containing head and body sections, with a link element pointing to a style sheet
<html lang="en">
<head>
<meta charset="UTF-8">
<title>Column Styling Example</title>
<link rel="stylesheet" href="column.css">
</head>
<body> <!-- Content to go here --> </body>
</html>

3 Within the body section, insert a table element that includes an identity for styling purposes and a caption
<table id="jfk">
<caption>Breakfast Flights</caption>
<!-- Table content to go here -->
</table>

4 Next in the table, insert a column group that includes a class name for styling and contains a single column
<colgroup class="sidebar">
<col>
</colgroup>

...cont'd

5 Now insert two more column groups that include class names for both group styling and individual styling
```
<colgroup class="info">
<col class="stripe"> <col> <col class="stripe"></colgroup>
<colgroup class="info">
<col> <col class="stripe"> </colgroup>
```

The **•** character entity is used in this table footer to create bullet points.

6 After the column groups insert a table header, a table footer, and a table body – each with six columns
```
<thead><tr><th colspan="6"><!-- Header --></thead>
<tfoot><tr><td colspan="6"><!-- Footer --></tfoot>
<tbody><!-- Rows with six cells each --></tbody>
```

7 Create a style sheet with rules to specify the appearance of the table, and its header, footer, and data cells
```
table#jfk { width : 580px ; border-collapse : collapse ; }
table#jfk tbody th { background : blue ; color : white ; }
table#jfk tbody td { padding : 3px ; text-align : center ; }
table#jfk tfoot { font-size : small ; }
```

column.css

8 Next add rules to specify the width of each column
```
table#jfk colgroup.sidebar col { width : 70px ; }
table#jfk colgroup.info col { width : 80px ; }
```

9 Now add rules to style groups and individual columns
```
table#jfk colgroup.info { border-left : 2px solid white ; }
table#jfk colgroup col.stripe { background : aqua ; }
```

10 Save the HTML document and style sheet then open the web page in your browser to see how the column groups and individual columns are now distinct from each other

column.html	Column Styling Example				
Breakfast Flights New York (JFK) - Los Angeles (LAX)					
	American Airlines	Delta Air Lines	Alaska Airlines	United	Continental
Departure	08:30	07:00	07:30	07:55	08:35
Arrival	12:05	10:30	10:45	11:30	12:00
Duration	6h35min	6h30min	6h15min	6h35min	6h25min
Price	$179	$195	$235	$225	$189

• Flights are Non-Stop • Times are Local • Tickets are 1-Way • Prices Include Tax

Summary

- The HTML5 **<ul>** element creates an unordered bullet-point list that contains individual list items within **<li>** elements

- A **list-style-type** property can specify that unordered list items should have a **disc, circle,** or **square** bullet-point, or **none**

- A **list-style-image** property can specify the URL of an image that should appear in place of list item bullet-points

- The **<ol>** element creates an ordered numerical list that contains individual list items within **<li>** elements

- A **list-style-type** property can specify how ordered list items should be numbered, such as **decimal, upper-latin,** or **none**

- The **<dl>** element creates a definition list containing terms in **<dt>** elements and their descriptions in **<dd>** elements

- The HTML5 **<table>** element creates a table and may optionally first enclose a **<caption>** element to title the table

- Each table row is created with a **<tr>** element to contain numerous **<th>** heading elements and **<td>** data elements

- Table cells can span down other cells using the **rowspan** attribute and cells to the right using the **colspan** attribute

- Adding **<thead>** and **<tfoot>** elements, immediately after the **<caption>** element, enhances a table with a header and footer

- Tables that have a header and footer must also enclose all regular table rows within a **<tbody>** element

- A table cell's **text-align** and **vertical-align** properties can be used to specify its content's horizontal and vertical alignment

- Table columns can be grouped using a **<colgroup>** element to specify the number of columns to group with its **span** attribute

- Each table column can be represented by a **<col>** element so it can be individually styled

7 Embedding media content

This chapter demonstrates how to create content-rich web pages by embedding media objects within HTML5 documents.

Embedding objects

An external resource can be embedded into an HTML5 document using **<object>** **</object>** tags to define the resource. When the resource is an image it will be treated much like those specified by **<img>** elements, otherwise a plugin may be sought to process the resource. The **<object>** element can specify the resource's URL to its **data** attribute and the resource type to its **type** attribute. The resource type must be a valid MIME type describing the resource.

MIME Type:	Object File Format:
image/png	PNG image resource
image/jpeg	JPG, JPEG, JPE image resource
image/gif	GIF image resource
image/svg+xml	SVG vector image resource
text/plain	TXT regular plain text resource
text/html	HTM, HTML markup text resource
application/pdf	PDF portable document resource
application/msword	DOC Word document resource
application/x-java-applet	CLASS Java applet resource
audio/x-wav	WAV sound resource
audio/mpeg	MP3 music resource
video/mp4	MP4 video resource
video/x-mpeg	MPEG, MPG, MPE video resource
video/x-msvideo	AVI video resource
video/x-msv-wmv	WMV Windows video resource
video/quicktime	MOV Quicktime video resource

This table lists some popular MIME types. Further details can be found on the W3C website at **www.w3.org**.

120

Beware

All **<object>** elements must contain at least one **data** attribute or one **type** attribute.

Each **<object>** element can specify dimensions in which to display visual content using its **width** and **height** attributes. Where the resource is an image the **<object>** element can also include a **usemap** attribute to specify the name of an image map, just like those produced for an **<img>** element.

Optionally, fallback text can be included between the **<object>** **</object>** tags that will only be displayed by the browser in the event that the resource cannot be embedded within the document. For example, when an appropriate plugin cannot be found.

...cont'd

1 Start with the HTML5 document type declaration
```
<!DOCTYPE HTML>
```

pdf.html

2 Add a root element containing head and body sections
```
<html lang="en">
<head>
<meta charset="UTF-8">
<title>Embedding PDF Example</title>
</head>
<body> <!-- Content to go here --> </body>
</html>
```

3 Within the body section, insert a paragraph wrapper
```
<p>This is text in the main document that...<br>
<!-- Resource to be embedded here -->
<br>...continues around an embedded resource.</p>
```

4 Within the paragraph, insert a PDF object to embed
```
<object data="piechart.pdf" type="application/pdf"
        width="580" height="310">
[ PDF Document - Requires Adobe Reader Plugin ]
</object>
```

piechart.pdf
(external resource)

5 Save the HTML document alongside the specified
resource file then open the web page to see it embedded

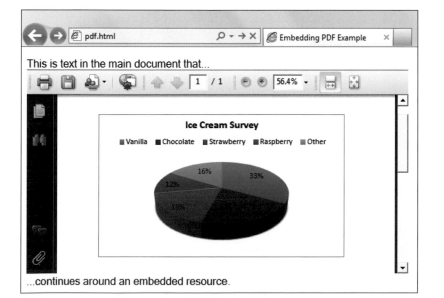

Hot tip

Disable plugin support
then re-open this
example to see the
fallback text appear in
place of the embedded
PDF document.

Embedding with parameters

Some external resources embedded into an HTML5 document can be passed "parameter" values to the plugin processing that resource to control its execution. For example, a plugin's "autoplay" property might be passed a "false" value to suppress automatic playback when the resource gets embedded into the web page.

An appropriate plugin will be sought after the resource type is identified by the MIME type specified to an **<object>** element's **type** attribute. Parameter values for that particular plugin can then be specified using **<param>** elements nested between the **<object> </object>** tags. Each **<param>** element must have both a **name** attribute and a **value** attribute, which pass the parameters to the plugin as a name/value pair. For example, automatic playback might be suppressed with this element:

<param name="autoplay" value="false">

The permissible parameter names and values are specific to each object but are given in their documentation. For example, the permissible parameter names and values for Java applets are provided in each applet's documentation – as they have been specified by the applet creator to suit that particular application. In this case the Java Runtime Environment (JRE) uses the parameters specified in each **<param>** element to control execution of the applet.

applet.html

1 Start with the HTML5 document type declaration
<!DOCTYPE HTML>

2 Add a root element containing head and body sections
<html lang="en">
<head>
<meta charset="UTF-8">
<title>Embedding Applet Example</title>
</head>
<body> <!-- Content to go here --> **</body>**
</html>

3 Within the body section, insert a paragraph wrapper
**<p>This is text in the main document that...
**
<!-- Resource to be embedded here -->
**
...continues around an embedded resource.</p>**

...cont'd

4 Within the paragraph, insert an applet object to embed
```
<object type="application/x-java-applet"
                width="580" height="300">
[ Java Applet - Requires Java Runtime Environment (JRE) ]
</object>
```

5 Before the fallback text within the object element, insert a parameter specifying the applet resource's URL
```
<param name="code" value="barchart.class">
```

barchart.class
(external resource)

6 Next within the object element, insert parameters defining data to be used by this particular applet
```
<param name="title" value="Web Browser Popularity">

<param name="val_1" value="45">
<param name="description_1" value="Internet Explorer">
<param name="val_2" value="35">
<param name="description_2" value="Firefox">
<param name="val_3" value="10">
<param name="description_3" value="Google Chrome">
<param name="val_4" value="6">
<param name="description_4" value="Safari">
<param name="val_5" value="4">
<param name="description_5" value="Opera">
```

7 Save the HTML document alongside the specified resource file then open the web page to see it embedded

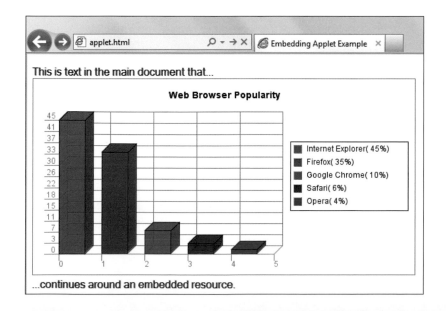

Beware

If fallback text is included it should appear just before the closing **</object>** tag.

Embedding in frames

External resources can be embedded in an HTML5 document within an "inline frame" using **<iframe> </iframe>** tags. These create a fixed area on the page in which to display the embedded resource. The inline frame's dimensions must be specified to the **<iframe>** element's **width** and **height** attributes and the URL of the external resource to its **src** attribute. Where the dimensions of the external resource exceed those of the inline frame the browser automatically adds scroll bars so the user can view the entire content.

Each **<iframe>** element may also optionally contain a **name** attribute to specify a unique identifier for that frame. This allows hyperlinks to then load the URL specified to their **href** attribute into the inline frame (rather than replace the entire page) by assigning the frame name to a **target** attribute in the **<a>** element. For example, a hyperlink could target an inline frame named "topbox" with **<a href="some.html" target="topbox">**.

Typically inline frames are useful to provide supplemental content while maintaining a compact page format.

iframe.html

A fallback message can be provided between the **<iframe> </iframe>** tags to be displayed when inline frame support is disabled.

1. Start with the HTML5 document type declaration
<!DOCTYPE HTML>

2. Add a root element containing head and body sections, with a link element pointing to a style sheet
<html lang="en">
<head>
<meta charset="UTF-8">
<title>Inline Frame Example</title>
<link rel="stylesheet" href="iframe.css">
</head>
<body> <!-- Content to go here --> </body>
</html>

3. Within the body section, insert an article containing a heading and descriptive paragraph, and with a specified class name for positional styling purposes
<article class="left220">
<h3>Concept Cars</h3>
<p>Many of the creative and innovative concept cars premiered at the recent motor show left the audience in eager anticipation of their production.</p>
</article>

4 Next in the body, as an aside, insert an inline frame to load a document containing relevant text and illustrative photographs positioned horizontally side-by-side

```
<aside>
<iframe src="concept.html" width="300" height="200">
[ Framed Document - Requires Iframe Support ]
</iframe>
</aside>
```

concept.html
(external resource)

5 Now create a style sheet to size the article and position it to the left of the inline frame

```
article.left220
{ width : 220px ; float : left ; margin-right : 20px ; }
```

iframe.css

6 Save the HTML document and style sheet then open the web page to see the article and the inline frame content

7 Drag the inline frame's horizontal scrollbar to reveal the rest of the embedded document's content

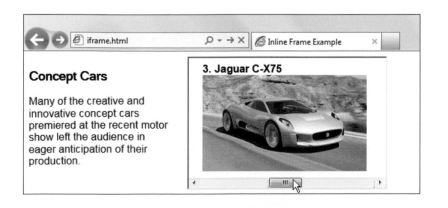

Hot tip

Embedding documents within inline frames is particularly favored on property websites to accompany property descriptions with photographs in a compact page format.

125

Embedding plugin movies

The **<object>** and **<iframe>** elements, described in the previous examples, can be used to embed other documents into a web page. External resources that provide interactive content, such as Flash "movies", can more easily be embedded by an **<embed>** element.

Each **<embed>** tag should specify the URL of the external interactive resource to its **src** attribute. For a Flash movie this will be the location of the ShockWave Flash (SWF) file. In order for the browser to seek an appropriate plugin the movie's MIME type should also be specified to its **type** attribute. For a Flash movie this will be "application/x-shockwave-flash". Additionally the dimensions of the area in which to display the movie on the page are specified to **width** and **height** attributes.

Web browsers that support HTML5 also support Scalable Vector Graphics (SVG). Unlike bitmap graphic formats such as PNG, which store their graphic information as the color of each pixel, vector graphics store the graphic information as a series of "paths". This is a highly efficient way to describe graphics. Most importantly vector graphics can be scaled without loss of fidelity. This means that they can be infinitely enlarged without suffering the pixelation experienced when enlarging bitmap images.

Hot tip

Static SVG images can be embedded using the **<img>** element – just like any other image.

SVG Vector X3   PNG Bitmap X3

SVG is not actually part of HTML5 but is a specification based on the eXtensible Markup Language (XML), so it describes vector images in text files. These can be created manually but it's far simpler to use a vector graphics editor such as Adobe Illustrator.

Just as Flash movies incorporate ActionScript for functionality SVG can incorporate JavaScript to create interactive SVG movies. These can be embedded in HTML5 by specifying the MIME type "image/svg+xml" to the **<embed>** element's **type** attribute.

...cont'd

1 Start a new HTML5 document
```
<!DOCTYPE HTML>
<html lang="en">
<head> <meta charset="UTF-8">
<title>Embedding Movie Example</title>
</head>
<body> <!-- Content to go here --> </body>
</html>
```

movie.html

2 In the body section, insert elements to embed two movies
```
<embed src="movie.swf" width="270" height="202"
                type="application/x-shockwave-flash" >
<embed src="movie.svg" width="285" height="205"
                type="image/svg+xml" >
```

movie.swf   movie.svg
(external resources)

3 Save the HTML document then open the web page in your browser to see the embedded movies

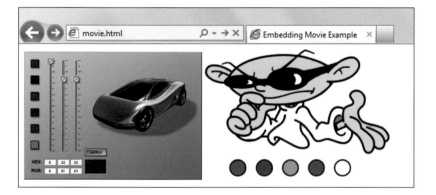

4 Select fill colors to interact with each embedded movie

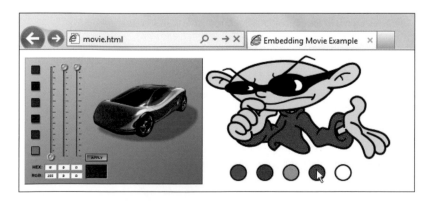

127

Don't forget

You can examine how JavaScript has been incorporated into this SVG document by downloading the examples archive from the Resource Center at **www.ineasysteps.com**.

Embedding audio

External audio resources, such as MP3 music files, can be embedded in an HTML5 document using **<audio> </audio>** tags.

The **<audio>** element can include a **src** attribute, to specify the URL of the audio resource to embed, and may include additional attributes to determine how the audio resource will be used:

- **autoplay** – a boolean attribute that specifies the browser should immediately begin playing the audio resource

- **loop** – a boolean attribute that specifies the browser should play the audio resource repeatedly

- **controls** – a boolean attribute that specifies the browser should display user controls to start and stop the audio playing

- **preload** – accepts values of "auto" or "none" to suggest the browser should load the audio resource so it is ready to play

Boolean attributes, like the **autoplay**, **loop**, and **controls** attributes, need have no assigned value – their presence alone within the element is sufficient for the browser to understand their purpose.

Browsers rely upon an in-built "codec" (**co**der-**dec**oder) to decode audio resources so they can be played. Sadly not all browsers incorporate the same audio codec:

- **Advanced Audio Coding (AAC)** – codec "mp4a.40.2" used by Internet Explorer, Safari, and Google Chrome for MP3 audio

- **Ogg audio** – codec "vorbis" used by Firefox, Opera, and again Google Chrome for audio files in OGG format

This inconsistency therefore requires audio resources to be encoded twice for playback across all browsers. Two **<source>** elements may be nested within an **<audio>** element for this purpose, rather than specifying a single resource URL to a **src** attribute in the **<audio>** tag. For each file format the **<source>** elements can then specify their resource URL to a **src** attribute, and their MIME type to a **type** attribute. The browser will only load the supported audio resource for playback.

Hot tip

A fallback message can be included between the **<audio> </audio>** tags to be displayed when audio playback support is disabled.

...cont'd

1 Start a new HTML5 document
```
<!DOCTYPE HTML>
<html lang="en">
<head> <meta charset="UTF-8">
<title>Audio Example</title>
</head>
<body> <!-- Content to go here --> </body>
</html>
```

audio.html

2 In the body section, insert an element to embed an audio resource in the MP3 format for automatic playback
```
<audio src="audio.mp3" autoplay > [ Fallback ] </audio>
```

audio.mp3 audio.ogg
(external resources)

3 Save the HTML document then open the web page with Internet Explorer, Safari, or Google Chrome to hear the audio playback – and Firefox or Opera to hear nothing

4 Next replace both previous attributes with one to display user controls for audio playback
```
<audio controls> <!-- Sources to go here --> </audio>
```

5 Now in the audio element, insert elements to specify audio resources to be embedded for all browsers
```
<source src="audio.mp3" type="audio/mpeg" >
<source src="audio.ogg" type="audio/ogg" >
```

6 Save the HTML document again, then open the web page in any browser and use the controls to hear playback

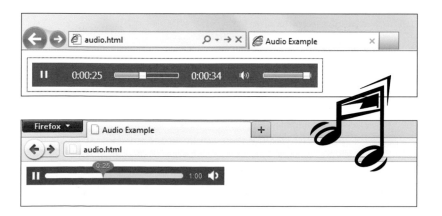

129

Embedding video

External video resources, such as MP4 video files, can be embedded in an HTML5 document using **\<video\> \</video\>** tags.

To determine how the video resource will be used the **\<video\>** element can include **src**, **autoplay**, **loop**, **controls**, and **preload** attributes, just like the **\<audio\>** element in the previous example. Additionally the dimensions of the area in which to display the video on the page can be specified to **width** and **height** attributes.

As with audio resources, browsers rely upon an in-built "codec" (**co**der-**dec**oder) to decode video resources so they can be played. Sadly not all browsers incorporate the same video codec:

● **Advanced Video Coding (AVC)** – codec "avc1.42E01E" used by Internet Explorer, Safari, and Google Chrome for MP4 video

● **Ogg video** – codec "theora" used by Firefox, Opera, and again Google Chrome for video files in OGV format

This inconsistency requires video resources to be encoded twice for playback across all browsers and embedded using two **\<source\>** elements nested within a **\<video\>** element. For each file format the **\<source\>** elements can then specify their resource URL to a **src** attribute and the MIME type of each video file can be specified to the **type** attribute. The browser will only load the supported video resource for playback.

Hot tip

The Advanced Video Coding standard is also often referred to by its project name of "H.264".

video.html

1 Start a new HTML5 document
```
<!DOCTYPE HTML>
<html lang="en">
<head> <meta charset="UTF-8">
<title>Video Example</title>
</head>
<body> <!-- Content to go here --> </body>
</html>
```

2 In the body section, insert an element to embed a video resource and display user controls for video playback
```
<video controls >
<!-- Sources to go here -->
[ Fallback ]
</video>
```

...cont'd

3 Next in the video element, insert an element to embed a video for Internet Explorer, Safari and Google Chrome
<source src="video.mp4" type="video/mp4" >

4 Now in the video element, insert an element to embed a video resource for the Firefox and Opera browsers
<source src="video.ogv" type="video/ogg" >

5 Save the HTML document then open the web page in any browser and use the controls to see video playback

video.mp4   video.ogv
(external resources)

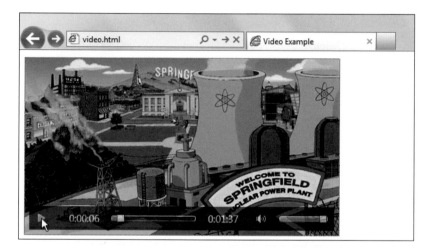

Providing offline access

Online HTML5 web applications can be made available offline by storing their components in the browser's "application cache". The component files to be stored must be listed in a "manifest" file that is specified to a **manifest** attribute in the **<html>** element. This may also list alternative fallback components for offline use.

The web application illustrated below comprises four components – **currency.html**, **currency.css**, **currency.png**, and a script **currency.js** that contains the latest exchange rates and advises so on the page.

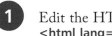

For offline use an alternative **currency-fallback.js** script can be specified in the manifest containing less generous exchange rates and advising that the web application is now using cached rates.

Don't forget

The files for this example, and all other examples in this book can be downloaded from the Resource Center at **www.ineasysteps.com**.

1 Edit the HTML5 document to specify a manifest
<html lang="en" manifest="currency.manifest">

2 Save the HTML document then create the manifest file in a text editor – exactly as listed below
CACHE MANIFEST
currency.html
currency.css
currency.png

FALLBACK:
currency.js currency-fallback.js

The files listed first are those to be stored in application cache. Notice that the online script is not included in that list, but the final line tells the browser to use the offline fallback script instead.

3 Manifests must have a **.manifest** file extension so save this one as "currency.manifest" then move all files to the server

currency.html

...cont'd

4 Manifests must only be served with the MIME type of **text/cache-manifest** so ensure the server is configured to associate this with the **.manifest** file extension

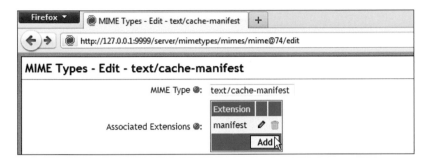

5 Open the application in your browser, via the web server, to see it appear as shown opposite – this will load the resources specified in the manifest into application cache

6 Disconnect from the network to go offline

7 Now empty your browser cache in the normal manner – this will only empty the local cache, not application cache

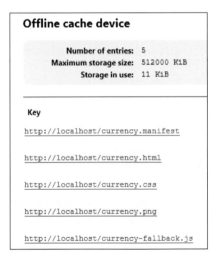

Offline cache device

Number of entries: 5
Maximum storage size: 512000 KiB
Storage in use: 11 KiB

Key

http://localhost/currency.manifest

http://localhost/currency.html

http://localhost/currency.css

http://localhost/currency.png

http://localhost/currency-fallback.js

8 Reload the application to see it is now available offline

133

Summary

- The HTML5 **<object> </object>** tags can be used to embed external resources within an HTML document

- An **<object>** tag can include **width** and **height** attributes to specify the size of a display area on the web page, a **data** attribute to specify the URL of an external resource, and a **type** attribute to specify the resource's MIME type

- Multiple **<param>** elements can be nested within an **<object>** element to specify parameters to **name** and **value** attributes

- External resources can be embedded into an inline frame within an HTML document using **<iframe> </iframe>** tags

- An **<iframe>** element can include **width** and **height** attributes to specify the size of a display area on the web page, and a **name** attribute so it can become the target of a hyperlink

- Each **<object>** and **<iframe>** element can include fallback text to be displayed when the resource cannot be embedded

- External resources can be embedded into an HTML document using **<embed>** tags

- An **<embed>** tag can include **width** and **height** attributes to specify the size of a display area on the web page, a **src** attribute to specify the URL of an external resource, and a **type** attribute to specify the resource's MIME type

- External audio resources can be embedded into an HTML document using **<audio> </audio>** tags, and external video resources can be embedded using **<video> </video>** tags

- Each **<audio>** and **<video>** element should include nested **<source>** elements to specify the resource URL to their **src** attribute and its MIME type to their **type** attribute

- Online web applications can be made available offline by specifying the name of a manifest file to a **manifest** attribute within the document's opening **<html>** tag

8 Building input forms

This chapter demonstrates how to build web forms within HTML5 documents for the submission of data to a web server.

Submitting forms

Web page forms are built from a number of HTML5 component elements that submit data to a web server for processing. Each of these elements include a **name** attribute and a **value** attribute so the data assigned to these attributes can be processed by the associated name=value pairs. For example, where an element's **name** attribute is assigned "Brand" and its **value** attribute is assigned "Ford" the name=value pair represents the data as Brand=Ford.

All form components are enclosed between **<form> </form>** tags. Each opening **<form>** tag should include a **method** attribute, specifying which HTTP method is to be used to submit the form, and an **action** attribute specifying the URL of a web server script that is to be used to process the submitted data.

The **method** attribute can be assigned values of "GET" or "POST". Submission via the preferred GET method appends the data to the URL, whereas submission via the POST method encodes the data differently and can be used when the GET method fails.

Typically an HTML form will have a "Submit" button that the user clicks to submit data for processing. This is created by assigning the value "submit" to a **type** attribute of an **<input>** tag. Additionally this tag may include **name** and **value** attributes to submit data assigned to them as a name=value pair.

In order to demonstrate form submission and web server response the examples throughout this chapter use a personal web server. This emulates submission of data to an external web server but is installed locally on the host computer. Like many web servers it has a directory named "htdocs" in which to deposit web pages and can be addressed by the domain name "localhost", or alternatively by the IP address "127.0.0.1". For example, to view the default web page entitled "index.html" with the server running you can enter **http://localhost/index.html** in the browser address field, or alternatively enter **http://127.0.0.1/index.html**.

To provide a response from the web server the **htdocs** directory contains a custom server-side script named "echo.pl" that echos the submitted name=value data in a HTML response document – in each example its URL is assigned to the form's **action** attribute. The web server's response simply displays the submitted values in a table to confirm the form data was received.

The examples in this chapter use the free Abyss Personal Edition web server available from **www.aprelium.com**.

The server-side scripts used to process the examples in this chapter are written in the Perl language and require the installation of ActivePerl support on Windows systems. This can be freely downloaded from **www.activestate.com**.

...cont'd

1 Start a new HTML5 document
```
<!DOCTYPE HTML>
<html lang="en">
<head>
<meta charset="UTF-8">
<title>Form Submission Example</title>
</head>
<body> <!-- Content to go here --> </body>
</html>
```

submit.html

2 In the body section, insert an element to submit form data to a server-side script using the GET method
```
<form method="GET" action="http://localhost/echo.pl" >
<!-- Form components to go here -->
</form>
```

3 Now in the form element, insert a paragraph containing a submission button – whose value will appear on the button
```
<p>
<input type="submit"
        name="My Submit Button Name"
        value="My Submit Button Value">
</p>
```

4 Save the HTML document then open the web page in your browser and click the button to submit the data assigned to its name=value pair, and to see the response

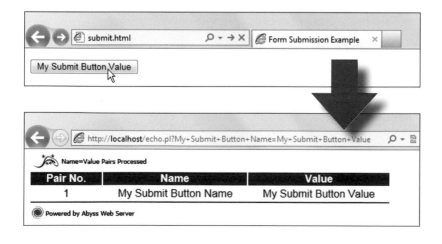

Beware

To process the examples in this chapter the files **echo.pl**, **echo.css**, **perl.png**, **abyss.png** should be placed in the "htdocs" directory of a local running web server – these are located in the download archive for this book available from the Resource Center at **www.ineasysteps.com**.

Don't forget

Notice the data appended in the browser's address field by the GET method – you can submit via the POST method to prevent this for sensitive data.

Gathering text input

An HTML5 form can provide text boxes where the user can input data for submission to the web server for processing. These are created by assigning the value "text" to the **type** attribute of an **<input>** tag and a name to its **name** attribute. Upon submission the data in the text box is sent as the value associated with the text box name as a name=value pair. Optionally the **<input>** tag can include a **value** attribute to specify a default value.

A text box for the input of a password is created by assigning the value "password" to the **type** attribute of an **<input>** tag. This functions just like any other text box except it does not display its contents as readable text.

Both password and regular text **<input>** elements can optionally include a number of other attributes to control their performance:

- **size** – the width of the text box in average character widths

- **maxlength** – the maximum number of characters permissible

- **readonly** – the default value in the text box cannot be changed

- **disabled** – the text box is grayed out and will not be submitted

text.html

1 Start a new HTML5 document
```
<!DOCTYPE HTML>
<html lang="en">
<head>
<meta charset="UTF-8">
<title>Text Input Example</title>
</head>
<body> <!-- Content to go here --> </body>
</html>
```

2 In the body section, insert a form element containing a submit button to send form data by the GET method
```
<form method="GET" action="http://localhost/echo.pl" >
<!-- Text input elements to go here -->
<p><input type="submit" value="Submit Form"></p>
</form>
```

3 Now in the form element, insert a definition list element
```
<dl>
<!-- Terms and descriptions to go here -->
</dl>
```

4 In the definition list, insert terms and descriptions
```
<dt>User Name :
<dd><input type="text" name="Name">
<dt>Password :
<dd><input type="password" name="Password">
<dt>City :
<dd><input type="text" name="City" value="Dallas">
<dt>Area :
<dd><input type="text" name="Area"
                    value="Downtown" disabled>
<dt>State :
<dd><input type="text" name="State"
                    value="Texas" readonly >
<dt>Zip Code :
<dd><input type="text" name="Zip Code"
                    size="5" maxlength="5">
```

5 Save the HTML document then open the web page in your browser, enter some data and submit the form

Hot tip

Notice that the **readonly** attribute ensures that the State cannot be edited, the **maxlength** attribute limits the Zip Code to 5 characters in length, and the **disabled** attribute grays out the Area text box – so that element will not be submitted to the server for processing.

139

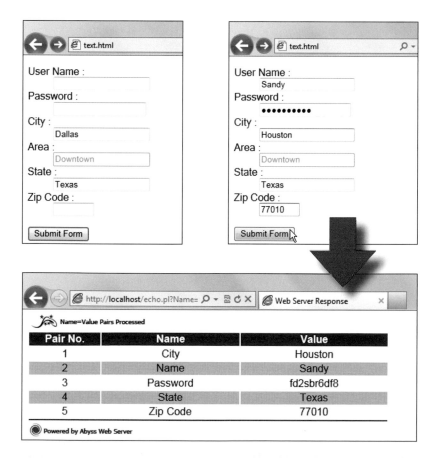

Pair No.	Name	Value
1	City	Houston
2	Name	Sandy
3	Password	fd2sbr6df8
4	State	Texas
5	Zip Code	77010

Powered by Abyss Web Server

Don't forget

The server-side script echos the name=value pairs arranged in alphabetical name order, irrespective of their order on the page.

Providing text areas

An HTML5 form can provide a multi-line text field where the user can input data for submission to the web server for processing. These are created by **<textarea> </textarea>** tags that may enclose default text content. The **<textarea>** tag should include a **name** attribute that will be associated with the element's content upon submission as a name=value pair. Additionally this tag must include a **rows** attribute, to specify the number of visible text lines, and a **cols** attribute to specify the field width in average character widths. Optionally it may also include a **readonly** attribute to prevent the user editing its content.

When submitting large bodies of text you must be aware of some limitations of the GET method. This varies by browser but Internet Explorer typically allows the URL to append up to around 200 characters. The POST method provides much larger capacity as the text is sent as "Form Data" along with the HTTP header, not simply appended to the URL:

Don't forget

Unlike a text **<input>** element the **<textarea>** element has no **value** attribute – as its content is treated as its value.

textarea.html

1 Start a new HTML5 document
```
<!DOCTYPE HTML>
<html lang="en">
<head>
<meta charset="UTF-8">
<title>Text Area Example</title>
</head>
<body> <!-- Content to go here --> </body>
</html>
```

2 In the body section, insert a form element containing a submit button to send form data by the POST method
```
<form method="POST" action="http://localhost/echo.pl" >
<!-- Text area element to go here -->
<p><input type="submit" value="Submit Form"></p>
</form>
```

3 Now in the form element, insert a text input area that has 10 rows and is 65 average character widths wide
```
<textarea name="The Future Web"
                    rows="10" cols="65">

</textarea>
```

4 Save the HTML document then open the web page in your browser, enter some data and submit the form

...cont'd

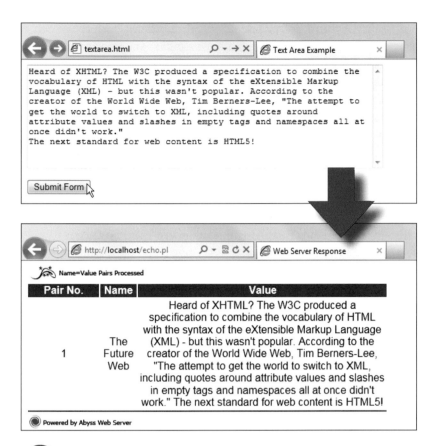

Beware

The average character width may vary between browsers – so the physical size of the text area field may vary too.

5 The text is not appended to the URL, so examine the response headers to see it has been sent as "Form Data"

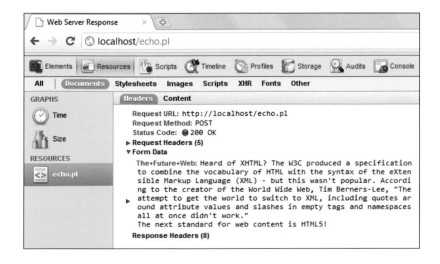

Hot tip

You can use the Developer Tools in the Google Chrome web browser to examine response headers – as illustrated here.

Checking boxes

An HTML5 form can provide a visual checkbox "on/off" switch that the user can toggle to include or exclude its associated data for submission to the server. When the box is checked the switch is set to "on" and its name=value pair will be submitted, but when the box is unchecked the switch is set to "off" and its name=value pair is not submitted.

A checkbox is created by assigning the value "checkbox" to the **type** attribute of an **<input>** tag. This tag must also include a **name** attribute and a **value** attribute to specify the name=value pair values. Optionally this tag may also include a boolean **checked** attribute to set the initial state of the switch to "on" – so a check mark will automatically appear in the checkbox.

Checkbox names may be individually unique or several checkboxes can share a common name to allow the user to select multiple values for the same named property. In this case the selected values are returned by the server as a comma-separated list where name=value,value,value.

Multiple checkboxes that share a common name can be visually grouped by surrounding their **<input>** elements by **<fieldset>** **</fieldset>** tags. These may also contain **<legend>** **</legend>** tags to contain a common group name:

Beware

The **<fieldset>** element only groups the related elements it encloses for visual presentation – it does not associate them programatically.

checkbox.html

1 Start a new HTML5 document
```html
<!DOCTYPE HTML>
<html lang="en">
<head>
<meta charset="UTF-8">
<title>Checkbox Example</title>
</head>
<body> <!-- Content to go here --> </body>
</html>
```

2 In the body section, insert a form element containing a submit button to send form data by the GET method
```html
<form method="GET" action="http://localhost/echo.pl" >
<!-- Checkbox elements to go here -->
<p>
<input type="submit" value="Submit Form">
</p>
</form>
```

3 Now in the form element, insert a paragraph containing a checkbox to appear automatically checked
<p>Yes, I would like to receive details
<input type="checkbox"
   name="Ask For" value="Details" checked></p>

4 Next in the form element, insert a fieldset containing a legend and five checkboxes to appear unchecked
<fieldset>
<legend>Activities of Interest...</legend>
Sailing <input type="checkbox" name="Do" value="Sail">
**
**
Walking <input type="checkbox" name="Do" value="Walk">
**
**
Driving <input type="checkbox" name="Do" value="Drive">
**
**
Ski-ing <input type="checkbox" name="Do" value="Ski">
**
**
Jogging <input type="checkbox" name="Do" value="Jog">
</fieldset>

5 Save the HTML document then open the web page in your browser, check some boxes, and submit the form

Notice that the **checked** attribute need have no assigned value – its mere presence sets the switch to "on" and its absence leaves the switch in its default "off" state.

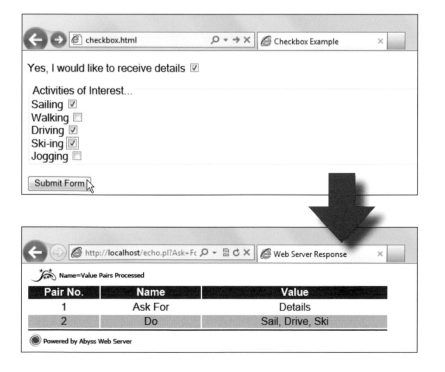

As the checkboxes for the Walking and Jogging activities are unchecked their name=value pairs are not sent to the server.

Pair No.	Name	Value
1	Ask For	Details
2	Do	Sail, Drive, Ski

Powered by Abyss Web Server

Choosing radio buttons

An HTML5 form can provide visual "radio button" groups, from which the user can select one button to include its associated data for submission to the server. When the button is selected its switch is set to "on" and its name=value pair will be submitted, otherwise its switch is set to "off" and its name=value pair is not submitted. Unlike checkboxes, radio buttons that share a common name are mutually exclusive, so when one radio button is selected all others in that group are automatically switched off.

A radio button is created by assigning the value "radio" to the **type** attribute of an **<input>** tag. This tag must also include a **name** attribute and a **value** attribute to specify the name=value pair values. Optionally this tag may also include a boolean **checked** attribute to set the initial state of the switch to "on" – so the button will automatically appear selected.

Radio button groups that share a common name can be visually grouped by surrounding their **<input>** elements by **<fieldset>** **</fieldset>** tags. These may also contain **<legend>** **</legend>** tags to contain a group name:

radio.html

1 Start a new HTML5 document
```
<!DOCTYPE HTML>
<html lang="en">
<head>
<meta charset="UTF-8">
<title>Radio Button Example</title>
</head>
<body> <!-- Content to go here --> </body>
</html>
```

2 In the body section insert a form element containing a submit button to send form data by the GET method
```
<form method="GET" action="http://localhost/echo.pl" >
<p>Choose only one answer...</p>
<!-- Fieldset to go here -->
<p> <input type="submit" value="Submit Form"> </p>
</form>
```

3 Next in the form element, insert a fieldset with a legend
```
<fieldset>
<legend>What kind of language is HTML?</legend>
<!-- Radio button elements to go here -->
</fieldset>
```

...cont'd

4 Now in the fieldset, insert radio buttons with one selected
```
Scripting <input type="radio"
        name="Definition" value="Scripting">
<br>
Markup <input type="radio"
        name="Definition" value="Markup">
<br>
Programming <input type="radio"
name="Definition" value="Programming" checked>
```

5 Save the HTML document then open the web page, select the correct answer, and submit the form

Always include a **checked** attribute to automatically select one button in each radio button group – to provide a default choice.

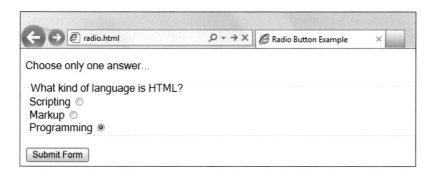

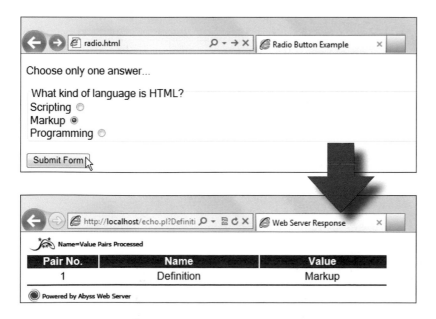

Radio button elements resemble the buttons on old radios where each button selected a particular radio station – but, of course, no two stations could be selected simultaneously.

Selecting options

An HTML5 form can provide a select option list, from which the user can select one option to include its associated data for submission to the server.

A select option list is created using **<select> </select>** tags. The opening **<select>** tag must include a **name** attribute specifying a list name. The **<select>** element encloses **<option> </option>** tags that define each option. Each opening **<option>** tag must include a **value** attribute specifying an option value. When the form is submitted the list name and the selected option value are sent to the server as a name=value pair.

Optionally one **<option>** tag may also include a boolean **selected** attribute to automatically select that option and the **<option>** elements may be grouped by enclosure in **<optgroup> </optgroup>** tags. The opening **<optgroup>** tag may specify an option group name to a **label** attribute.

A select option list will normally appear as a single-line dropdown list unless a **size** attribute is included in the **<select>** tag to specify the number of rows to be visible:

select.html

1 Start a new HTML5 document
```
<!DOCTYPE HTML>
<html lang="en">
<head>
<meta charset="UTF-8">
<title>Select Option Example</title>
</head>
<body> <!-- Content to go here --> </body>
</html>
```

2 In the body section insert a form element containing a submit button to send form data by the GET method
```
<form method="GET" action="http://localhost/echo.pl" >
<!-- Select option lists to go here -->
<p>
<input type="submit" value="Submit Form">
</p>
</form>
```

3 Now in the form element, insert a fixed height select option list with one option automatically selected

```
<select name="HTML List Type Selector One" size="4">
<optgroup label="List Type 1">
<option value="UL">Unordered List</option>
<option value="OL" selected>Ordered List</option>
<option value="DL">Definition List</option>
</optgroup>
</select>
```

Hot tip

Always include a **selected** attribute to automatically select one option in each option list – to provide a default choice.

4 Next in the form element, insert a dropdown select option list with one option automatically selected

```
<select name="HTML List Type Selector Two">
<optgroup label="List Type 2">
<option value="UL">Unordered List</option>
<option value="OL">Ordered List</option>
<option value="DL" selected>Definition List</option>
</optgroup>
</select>
```

5 Save the HTML document then open the web page in your browser, open the dropdown list and submit the form to see the default option values get submitted

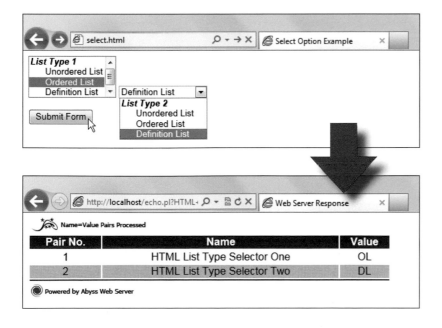

Utilizing hidden data

The form elements introduced in previous examples create visible "controls" that allow the user to manually enter or select data for submission to the server. An HTML5 form can also provide hidden elements, that create no visible controls, which allow static or script-generated data to be submitted to the server.

Hidden form data is created by assigning the value "hidden" to the **type** attribute of an **<input>** tag. This tag must also include a **name** attribute and may include a **value** attribute to specify static data that will be submitted as a name=value pair. Optionally the **<input>** tag may include an **id** attribute and omit the **value** attribute so its value can be specified by script. For example, static data could identify a form number and scripting could identify the user's browser and submission date:

hidden.html

1 Start a new HTML5 document that incorporates a script
```
<!DOCTYPE HTML>
<html lang="en">
<head>
<meta charset="UTF-8">
<title>Hidden Data Example</title>
<script src="hidden.js"> </script>
</head>
<body> <!-- Content to go here --> </body>
</html>
```

2 In the body section insert a form element containing a submit button to send form data by the GET method
```
<form method="GET" action="http://localhost/echo.pl" >
<!-- Hidden data to go here -->
<input type="submit" value="Submit Form">
</form>
```

3 Within the form element, insert a visible input element for user-entered data
```
User Name: <input type="text" name="Name">
```

4 Next in the form element, insert an invisible element for hidden static data
```
<input type="hidden" name="Form No." value="257">
```

Hot tip

Hidden data elements can be useful to maintain user data across a website – a user name entered on the first page can be recalled on any other page.

5 Now in the form element, insert two invisible elements for hidden script-generated data

```
<input type="hidden" name="Browser" id="Browser">
<input type="hidden" name="Date" id="Date">
```

6 Create a script to generate value attributes for two invisible form elements when the page gets loaded

```
function init()
{
  document.getElementById("Browser").value=
                          navigator.appName ;
  document.getElementById("Date").value=new Date() ;
}
onload=init ;
```

hidden.js

7 Save the HTML document and script then open the web page in your browser, enter data, and submit the form

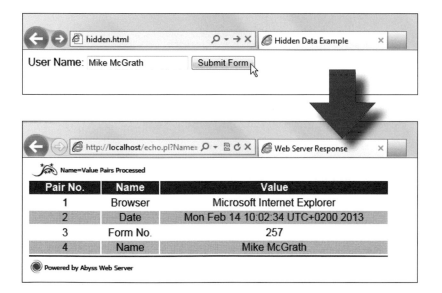

Pair No.	Name	Value
1	Browser	Microsoft Internet Explorer
2	Date	Mon Feb 14 10:02:34 UTC+0200 2013
3	Form No.	257
4	Name	Mike McGrath

Beware

JavaScript is case-sensitive so you must use the correct case when copying script examples.

Pushing buttons

An HTML5 form can provide push buttons for scripting purposes. When the user pushes a button a "click event" occurs to which a script function can respond. This allows the user to dynamically interact with the form and can be used to set attribute values. When a script designates a function to be called whenever a button gets pushed it is said to attach a "behavior" to that button. A push button is created by specifying a "button" value to the **type** attribute of an **<input>** tag and should also include an **id** attribute so the script can easily identify that element.

Additionally any HTML5 form can be returned to its original state by pushing a reset button that is created by specifying a "reset" value to the **type** attribute of an **<input>** tag:

button.html

1 Start a new HTML5 document that incorporates a script
```
<!DOCTYPE HTML>
<html lang="en">
<head>
<meta charset="UTF-8">
<title>Button Example</title>
<script src="button.js"> </script>
</head>
<body> <!-- Content to go here --> </body>
</html>
```

2 In the body section insert a form element containing a reset button, a push button, and a submit button to send form data by the GET method
```
<form method="GET" action="http://localhost/echo.pl" >
<!-- Fieldset to go here -->
<input type="reset" value="Reset Form">
<input type="button" value="Choose For Me" id="btn">
<input type="submit" value="Submit Form">
</form>
```

3 Within the form element, insert a fieldset containing a legend and a checkbox group
```
<fieldset>
<legend>Pizza Toppings</legend>
<input id="pepperoni" type="checkbox"
  name="Toppings" value="Pepperoni"> Pepperoni |
<input id="mushroom" type="checkbox"
  name="Toppings" value="Mushroom"> Mushroom |
<input id="bbqsauce" type="checkbox"
  name="Toppings" value="BBQ Sauce"> BBQ Sauce
</fieldset>
```

…cont'd

4 Create a script that designates a function when the page gets loaded to attach a behavior to the form's push button

button.js

```
function choose()
{ document.getElementById("pepperoni").checked=true ; }

function init()
{ document.getElementById("btn").onclick=choose ; }

onload=init;
```

5 Save the HTML document and script then open the web page in your browser, and push the button to check a box

6 Now push the reset button to clear the form, then check the other two boxes and submit the form

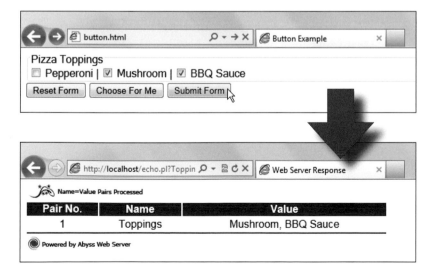

151

Don't forget

The mere presence of a boolean **checked** attribute in an HTML element checks the box, but in script the box's **checked** property needs to be assigned a **true** value to check the box.

Using images for submission

An HTML5 form can use an image button to submit the form, in place of a regular submit button. An image button is created by specifying an "image" value to the **type** attribute of an **<input>** tag and including an **alt** attribute. When a form is submitted by an image button the XY coordinates of the point at which the click occurred are automatically submitted as name=value pairs along with the rest of the form data.

Additionally, a regular **<img>** tag can be used as an image button by attaching a behavior with script. Where the behavior is to submit a form the script function can usefully incorporate validation. For example, to ensure a user-entered email address is in the expected format:

ibutton.html

1 Start a new HTML5 document that incorporates a script
```
<!DOCTYPE HTML>
<html lang="en">
<head>
<meta charset="UTF-8">
<title>Image Button Example</title>
<script src="ibutton.js"> </script>
</head>
<body> <!-- Content to go here --> </body>
</html>
```

Don't forget

Note that the image button that will perform validation is given an identity so script can attach a behavior to it.

2 In the body section insert a form element containing a text input field, which both have an identity for scripting
```
<form id="form-1"
        method="GET" action="http://localhost/echo.pl" >
Please Supply Your Email Address:
<input id="adr"
        name="Address" type="text" size="45"> <br>
<!-- Image Buttons to go here -->
</form>
```

3 Next in the form element, insert an image button that will simply submit the form
```
<input type="image" src="ibutton.png"
 alt="Submit Button" title="Click to submit form">
```

4 Now in the form element, insert an image button that will perform validation then submit the form
```
<img id="btn" src="ibutton.png" alt="Submit Button"
 title="Click to submit with JavaScript validation">
```

5 Create a script that designates a function when the page gets loaded – to attach a behavior to an image button

```
function send()
{
  var address = document.getElementById("adr").value ;
  var pattern=
/^([a-zA-Z0-9_.-])+@([a-zA-Z0-9_.-])+\.([a-zA-Z])+([a-zA-Z])+/ ;
  if( ! pattern.test(address) ) alert("Invalid Email Address") ;
  else document.getElementById("form-1").submit() ;
}

function init()
{ document.getElementById("btn").onclick=send ; }

onload=init;
```

ibutton.js

6 Save the HTML document and script then open the web page in your browser, enter an incomplete email address and submit the form using each button

7 When validation fails using the button with scripted behavior, complete the email address correctly then use the validating button again to submit the form successfully

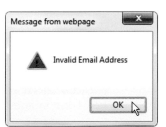

Beware

The script in this example checks the input text against a regular expression pattern that describes the format of any valid email address. The pattern must appear on a single line – exactly as it is listed here.

Adding logos to buttons

HTML5 can create push buttons that display small "logo" images using **\<button>** **\</button>** tags. These tags can then enclose an **\<img>** element specifying the URL of the logo image, and text that will appear on the face of the button. Each **\<button>** tag should include a **type** attribute to specify whether the button is simply a scripting "button" type, a "submit" form type, or a "reset" form type. Scripting buttons can include an **onclick** attribute in the **\<button>** tag to specify the function to be called when the button gets clicked, or directly specify a snippet of script to execute:

logo.html

1 Start a new HTML5 document
```
<!DOCTYPE HTML>
<html lang="en">
<head>
<meta charset="UTF-8">
<title>Logo Button Example</title>
</head>
<body> <!-- Content to go here --> </body>
</html>
```

2 In the body section, insert a form element containing a fieldset with a legend and a text input field
```
<form method="GET" action="http://localhost/echo.pl">
<fieldset>
<legend>Favorite Color</legend>
<input type="text" name="Color">
<!-- Logo Buttons to go here -->
</fieldset>
</form>
```

3 In the fieldset, insert a scripting logo button specifying a snippet of script to execute when that button gets clicked
```
<button type="button"
onclick="alert('Enter your favorite color in the text box')">
<!-- Logo Image and Face Text to go here --> </button>
```

4 Now within the button element, insert an image element and text that will appear on the face of the button
```
<img src="logo-help.png" alt="Help">Help
```

5 Next add a button element to submit the form
```
<button type="submit">
<img src="logo-submit.png" alt="Submit">
Submit</button>
```

...cont'd

6 Finally add a button element to reset the form
```
<button type="reset">
<img src="logo-reset.png" alt="Reset">Reset</button>
```

7 Save the HTML document then open the web page in your browser and click the "Help" button

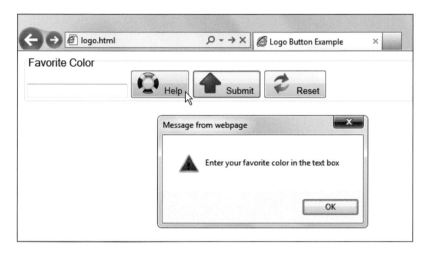

8 Enter a color in the text box, then click the reset logo button to clear the text box

9 Enter a color in the text box again then submit the form

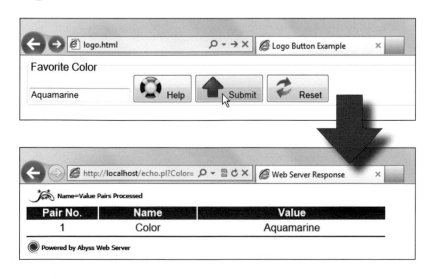

155

Don't forget

You can specify a default value for a text input to the **value** attribute of its **<input>** tag.

Labeling form controls

Text that is to be associated with an HTML5 form control can be enclosed between **<label>** **</label>** tags. The opening **<label>** tag can include a **for** attribute to specify the value assigned to the control's **id** attribute to make the association. Alternatively the **<label>** element can simply enclose both the text and the control element to make the association. This allows styling to be applied to the entire label – including the text and control. Often this is useful to distinguish the control associated with particular text.

Additionally each form control element may include a **tabindex** attribute to specify its tabbing order within the document as a unique value between 0 and 32,767. Using the tab key the user can then navigate through the document starting at the lowest **tabindex** value and proceeding through successively higher values:

label.html

156

1 Start a new HTML5 document with a link element pointing to a style sheet
```
<!DOCTYPE HTML>
<html lang="en">
<head>
<meta charset="UTF-8"> <title>Label Example</title>
<link rel="stylesheet" href="label.css">
</head>
<body> <!-- Content to go here --> </body>
</html>
```

Hot tip

A form "control" is any **<input>**, **<button>**, or **<textarea>** element. A **tabindex** attribute can be included in these tags and also in any **<a>**, **<area>**, **<object>**, or **<select>** tag.

2 In the body section, insert a form element containing a fieldset with a legend
```
<form method="GET" action="http://localhost/echo.pl">
<fieldset>
<legend>Toolbox</legend>
<!-- Form Controls to go here -->
</fieldset>
</form>
```

3 Now in the fieldset, insert labels that each contain text and a checkbox with a specified tab order
```
<label>Hammer
<input type="checkbox" name="Toolbox"
       value="Hammer" tabindex="2" checked></label>
<label>Wrench
<input type="checkbox" name="Toolbox"
       value="Wrench" tabindex="3"></label>

<!-- Three similar for tabindex 4,5,6 go here -->
```

...cont'd

4 Next in the fieldset, insert a logo submit button – to be first in the tab order
```
<button type="submit" tabindex="1">
<img src="toolbox.png">Submit</button>
```

5 Save the HTML document then open the web page in your browser to see the text-control association is unclear

6 Edit the HTML document to add a class attribute to each alternate label tag for styling purposes
```
<label class="hilite">
```

7 Create a style sheet with a rule to distinguish the labels
```
label.hilite { background : red ; color : white ; }
```

label.css

8 Save the HTML document and style sheet then open the web page to see that the text-control association is now clear. Use the tab key to move between controls and the space bar to select checkboxes, then submit the form

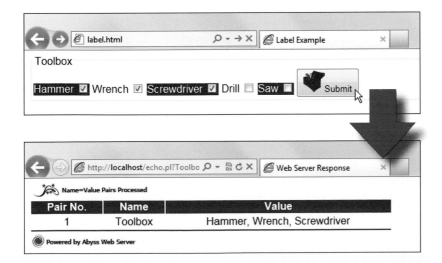

Uploading files

An HTML5 form can provide a file selection facility, which calls upon the operating system's "Choose File" dialog, to allow the user to browse their local file system and select a file.

A file selection facility is created by assigning the value "file" to the **type** attribute of an **<input>** tag and a name to its **name** attribute. This element produces a text field and a "Browse" button to launch the Choose File dialog. After a file has been selected its full path appears in the text field. When the form is submitted the element name and the selected file's name are sent to the web server as a name=value pair.

Where a selected file is to be uploaded to the web server the **<form>** tag must include an **enctype** attribute specifying the encoding type as "multipart/form-data". Also its **method** attribute must specify the POST method – because Form Data cannot be appended to a URL using the GET method:

upload.html

1 Start a new HTML5 document
```
<!DOCTYPE HTML>
<html lang="en">
<head>
<meta charset="UTF-8">
<title>File Upload Example</title>
</head>
<body> <!-- Content to go here --> </body>
</html>
```

2 In the body section insert a form element containing a submit button to send form data by the POST method and specify the encoding type for Form Data
```
<form method="POST" action="http://localhost/upload.pl"
        enctype="multipart/form-data">
<!-- File input element to go here -->
<input type="submit" value="Submit Form">
</form>
```

3 In the form element, insert a file element and a line break
```
<input type="file" name="Upload"> <br>
```

4 Save the HTML document then open the web page in your browser, select a file and submit the form

...cont'd

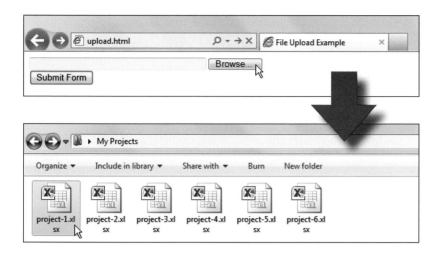

To process this example the files **upload.pl**, and **upload.css** need to be added to the "htdocs" directory of a local running web server – these are located in the download archive for this book available from the Resource Center at **www.ineasysteps.com**.

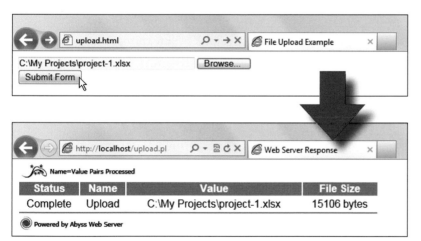

⑤ Examine the headers to see the file details as Form Data

Summary

- HTML5 forms submit data to the web server as name=value pairs for processing by a specified server-side script

- All form component elements are enclosed between **<form> </form>** tags, which must include an **action** attribute, to specify the URL of the processing script, and a **method** attribute to specify the submission method as "GET" or "POST"

- Each **<input>** tag must include a **type** attribute to specify its component type, such as "text", "password", "checkbox", "radio", "submit", "reset", "button", "hidden", "image", or "file"

- An **<input>** tag can include **name** and **value** attributes to specify data for submission as a name=value pair

- A multi-line text field is created by **<textarea> </textarea>** tags that require **rows** and **cols** attributes to specify its size

- Radio button and checkbox inputs only submit their **name** and **value** attribute data if they are checked

- An option list is created by enclosing a number of **<option>** elements between **<select> </select>** tags

- Option lists can be enclosed between **<optgroup> </optgroup>** tags that can specify a option group name to a **label** attribute

- Forms can contain "hidden" elements that allow static or script-generated data to be submitted to the server for processing

- A form may be submitted by a regular submit **<input>** element, by an image **<input>** element, or by a **<button>** element

- Logo images can be added to the button face by enclosing an **<img>** element between **<button> </button>** tags

- Each form control can be enclosed between **<label> </label>** tags to visually group them with text for styling purposes

- When a form is to upload files the **<form>** tag must include an **enctype** attribute specifying encoding as "multipart/form-data"

9 Painting on canvas

This chapter demonstrates how to dynamically paint images within an HTML5 document using JavaScript.

Generating a canvas

In HTML5 the **<canvas>** **</canvas>** tags create a bitmap canvas area on the page in which script can paint shapes and text. This can be used to dynamically generate graphs, game graphics, and visual images.

Initially the canvas area is invisible and will, by default, be 300 pixels wide and 150 pixels high. Alternative dimensions can be specified to the **<canvas>** element's **width** and **height** attributes.

Optionally fallback text can be included between the **<canvas>** **</canvas>** tags that will only be displayed by the browser in the event that the canvas area cannot be created.

In order to use the canvas a script must first create a "CanvasRenderingContext2D" object. This snappily named context object provides all the methods and properties needed to paint shapes and text in the canvas area. The context object is created using a **getContext()** method of the canvas itself. For example, for a **<canvas>** element with an **id** of "canvas" like this:

```
var canvas = document.getElementById( "canvas" ) ;
var context = canvas.getContext( "2d" ) ;
```

It is, however, good practice to first test for the existence of the canvas's **getContext()** method before creating the context object:

```
var canvas = document.getElementById( "canvas" ) ;
if ( canvas.getContext ) {  var context = canvas.getContext( "2d" ) ; }
```

Calls to the context object's methods, and assignments to its properties, can subsequently be added inside the **{ }** braces – to be implemented when the test succeeds.

A context object's **fillStyle** property can be assigned a color with which to paint a shape. For example, the context object's **fillRect()** method can be called to paint a rectangle with the assigned color. This method requires four comma-separated "arguments" within its **( )** parentheses – to specify the XY coordinate position on the canvas of the top left corner of the rectangle, its width, and its height:

context.**fillRect** (*x* , *y*, *width* , *height*) ;

Similarly, the context object's **clearRect()** method can be called to remove paint in a rectangle specified by the same four arguments:

context.**clearRect** (*x* , *y*, *width* , *height*) ;

Beware

JavaScript is case-sensitive so be sure to capitalize the **fillRect** and **clearRect** method names correctly – capital "R".

Don't forget

Canvas coordinates have their XY origin at their top left corner – so **fillRect(100,10, 50,50)** would paint a 50 pixel square 100 pixels from the left edge of the canvas and 10 pixels down from its top edge.

...cont'd

1 Start a new HTML5 document that incorporates a script and creates a canvas area of a specified size

canvas.html

```
<!DOCTYPE HTML>
<html lang="en">
<head>
<meta charset="UTF-8">
<title>Canvas Example</title>
<script src="canvas.js"></script>
</head>
<body>
<canvas id="canvas" width="550" height="150">
[Fallback Message]
</canvas>
</body>
</html>
```

2 Create a script with a function to paint the entire canvas area a specified color, then remove a 100-pixel square at specified coordinates, as soon as the document has loaded

canvas.js

```
function init()
{
  var canvas = document.getElementById( "canvas" ) ;
  if ( canvas.getContext )
  {
    var ctx = canvas.getContext( "2d" ) ;
    ctx.fillStyle = "#F30" ;
    ctx.fillRect ( 0, 0, canvas.width , canvas.height ) ;
    ctx.clearRect( 225, 25, 100,100 ) ;
  }
}
onload = init ;
```

Hot tip

3 Save the HTML document and script then open the web page in your browser to see the painted canvas area

Name the context object variable "ctx" for brevity as it will be typed often.

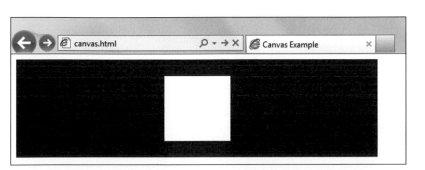

163

Painting shapes

The three basic shapes that can be painted on an HTML5 canvas are rectangle, circle, and polygon. A rectangle is the simplest shape to create using the context object's **fillRect()** method, introduced in the previous example, that has this syntax:

ctx.**fillRect (*x, y, width, height*) ;**

Creating circles and polygons requires a little more effort as they must both be initially created as a "path" describing the shape. The path of a circle describes the coordinates of its center point and its radius, and the path of a triangle describes the coordinates of each of its corners. A path always begins with a call to the context object's **beginPath()** method – announcing the creation of a path.

A circular path is created with the context object's **arc()** method whose arguments first describe the coordinates of its center point and its radius. Additionally, because this method can also be used to create a partial circle, further arguments describe the start angle, end angle, and the direction in which to paint:

ctx.**arc (*x, y, radius, startAngle, endAngle, direction*) ;**

Sadly the start and end angles must be specified in "radians", rather than degrees, but degrees can easily be converted to radians using the expression *degrees****Math.PI/180**. A complete circle of 360 degrees can therefore start at zero and end at **360*Math.PI/180**, more simply expressed as just **Math.PI*2**. The final argument to the context object's **arc()** method, describing the direction in which to paint, is a boolean value of either **true** or **false** – where **false** is clockwise and **true** is counterclockwise.

A polygonal path is created with the context object's **moveTo()** and **lineTo()** methods that both require two XY coordinate arguments. Initially the **moveTo()** method describes the point at which to begin the path, like lifting a pen off paper and moving to a new point at which to begin drawing. Successive calls to the **lineTo()** method then describe each corner point along the edge of the shape. Finally a call to the context object's **closePath()** method completes the path shape by returning to its starting point.

After creating a circular or polygonal path a simple call to the context object's **fill()** method will paint the shape with the color specified to the context object's current **fillStyle** property.

...cont'd

1 Create a script with a function to paint a 100-pixel square as soon as the document has loaded

shapes.js

```
function init()
{
  var canvas = document.getElementById( "canvas" ) ;
  if ( canvas.getContext )
  {
    var ctx = canvas.getContext( "2d" ) ;
    ctx.fillStyle = "#F30" ;
    ctx.fillRect ( 75, 10, 100 , 100 ) ;
    /*  More instructions go here */
  }
}
onload = init ;
```

2 Next insert instructions to paint a 50-pixel radius circle

```
ctx.fillStyle = "#3C0" ;
ctx.beginPath() ;
ctx.arc( 275, 60, 50, 0, Math.PI*2, true ) ;
ctx.fill() ;
```

3 Now insert instructions to paint a 100-pixel tall triangle

```
ctx.fillStyle = "#09F" ;
ctx.beginPath() ;
ctx.moveTo( 375, 110 ) ;
ctx.lineTo( 425,10 ) ;
ctx.lineTo( 475,110 ) ;
ctx.closePath() ;
ctx.fill() ;
```

4 Save the script alongside a HTML document that incorporates this script and creates a canvas with the id value of "canvas" (just like the one listed on page 163)

shapes.html

5 Open the web page in your browser to see the shapes get painted on the canvas

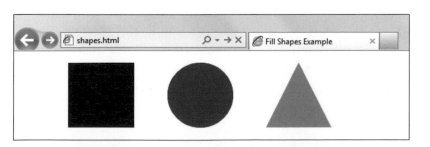

Stroking borders

Just as a context object provides a **fillStyle** property, **fillRect()** and **fill()** methods, that can be used to paint a shape, it also provides a **strokeStyle** property, **strokeRect()** and **stroke()** methods that can be used to paint borders.

The blue border shown here has 50% fill transparency to illustrate the overlap – setting fill transparency is described in the next example.

A context object's **strokeStyle** property can be assigned a color with which to paint the borders. The context object's **strokeRect()** method requires four comma-separated arguments within its ( ) parentheses – to specify the XY coordinate position on the canvas of the top left corner of a rectangle, its width and its height:

ctx.strokeRect (x, y, width, height) ;

Circular and polygonal borders are painted by first creating a path, as described in the previous example, then calling the context object's **stroke()** method.

Before painting a border, however, it is necessary to first specify a numeric pixel value to the context object's **lineWidth** property – to determine what brush width to use.

It should be noted that the border is painted of the specified **lineWidth** <u>centered</u> on the path – half outside and half inside. For example, with a **lineWidth** value of 20 pixels the border gets painted with 10 pixels on each side of the path:

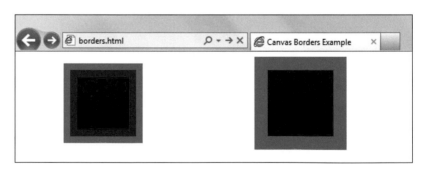

In order to paint a border entirely outside an existing fill path the stroke path width and height needs to be increased by the **lineWidth** value, and the XY coordinates need to be reduced by half the **lineWidth** value. For example, where the **lineWidth** value is 20 and the fill is created by **ctx.fillRect(20, 20, 100, 100)** an external border is created by **ctx.strokeRect(10, 10, 120, 120)**.

1 Create a script with a function to paint a 6-pixel wide border centered on a 100-pixel square path

stroke.js

```
function init()
{
  var canvas = document.getElementById( "canvas" ) ;
  if ( canvas.getContext )
  {
    var ctx = canvas.getContext( "2d" ) ;
    ctx.lineWidth = 6 ; ctx.strokeStyle = "#F30" ;
    ctx.strokeRect ( 75, 10, 100, 100 ) ;
    /*  More instructions go here */
  }
}
onload = init ;
```

2 Next insert instructions to paint a circular border

```
ctx.strokeStyle =" #3C0" ;
ctx.beginPath() ;
ctx.arc( 275, 60, 50, 0, Math.PI*2, true ) ;
ctx.stroke() ;
```

3 Now insert instructions to paint a triangular border

```
ctx.strokeStyle = "#09F" ;
ctx.beginPath() ;
ctx.moveTo( 375, 110 ) ;
ctx.lineTo( 425, 10 ) ;
ctx.lineTo( 475,110 ) ;
ctx.closePath() ;
ctx.stroke() ;
```

4 Save the script alongside a HTML document that incorporates this script and creates a canvas with the id value of "canvas" (just like the one listed on page 163)

stroke.html

5 Open the web page in your browser to see the borders get painted on the canvas

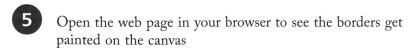

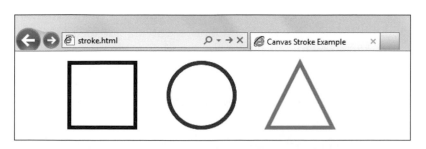

Filling options

Fill and stroke colors can be specified to a context object's **fillStyle** and **strokeStyle** properties as a recognized color name, such as "red", or as a hexadecimal value, such as "#FF0000" or its shorthand equivalent "#F00". Additionally colors can be specified by stating their red, green, and blue, component values in the range 0-255 with an **rgb()** expression. For example, the color red can be expressed as **rgb(255,0,0)** – having maximum red component value but no green or blue. The fill color's transparency can also be specified in the range 0.0-1.0 as the fourth argument in an **rgba()** expression. For example, the expression **rgba(255,0,0,0.5)** specifies maximum red of 50% transparency.

Alternatively a context object's **fillStyle** and **strokeStyle** properties can be assigned a "CanvasGradient" object that defines a multi-color gradient fill, in which one color gradually changes to another. To create a CanvasGradient object the context object provides two methods. The **createLinearGradient()** method requires four arguments to specify two XY coordinates at which to start and end a linear gradient. For example, **createLinearGradient(0,0,100,100)** defines a diagonal gradient from top left to bottom right. The **createRadialGradient()** method requires six arguments to specify two XY coordinates and two radius values at which to start and end a radial gradient. For example, **createRadialGradient(50,50,10,50,50,100)** defines a radial gradient between two circles centered at the same point.

Each CanvasGradient object has an **addColorStop()** method that requires two arguments to specify the position along the gradient in the range 0.0-1.0, and the color to paint at that position. For example, **addColorStop(0,"red")** begins the gradient fill with red and **addColorStop(1,"blue")** ends the gradient fill with blue.

A context object's **fillStyle** and **strokeStyle** properties can alternatively be assigned a "CanvasPattern" object that defines a pattern image and how it should be repeated. To create a CanvasPattern object the context object provides a **createPattern()** method. This requires two arguments specifying a loaded Image object and a repetition value of "repeat-x" (horizontal), "repeat-y" (vertical), or "repeat" (both). The Image object is simply created using the JavaScript **new Image()** constructor, then specifying the URL of an image to be used by the pattern to its **src** property.

Hot tip

Should you want to paint a lot of shapes with the same fill transparency you can specify a value in the range of 0.0-1.0 to the context object's **globalAlpha** property. For example, to set a 50% transparency with **ctx.globalAlpha=0.5**.

Beware

Do not simply specify the URL of an image as the first argument to the **createPattern()** method.

168

1 Create a script with a function to paint colored rectangles

```
function init()
{
  var canvas = document.getElementById( "canvas" ) ;
  if ( canvas.getContext )
  {
    var ctx = canvas.getContext( "2d" ) ;
    ctx.fillStyle = "rgb( 255, 51, 0 )" ;
    ctx.fillRect ( 50, 10, 80, 80 ) ;
    ctx.fillStyle = "rgba( 0, 153, 255, 0.5 )" ;
    ctx.fillRect( 100, 30, 80, 80 ) ;
    /*  More instructions go here */
  }
}
onload = init ;
```

options.js

2 Next insert instructions to paint gradient-filled rectangles

```
var linear = ctx.createLinearGradient( 0, 10, 0, 110 ) ;
linear.addColorStop( 0, "yellow" ) ;
linear.addColorStop( 1, "green" ) ;
ctx.fillStyle = linear ; ctx.fillRect( 200, 10, 100, 100 ) ;
var radial =
        ctx.createRadialGradient( 370, 60, 0, 370, 60, 70 ) ;
radial.addColorStop( 0, "yellow" ) ;
radial.addColorStop( 1, "green" ) ;
ctx.fillStyle = radial ; ctx.fillRect( 320, 10, 100, 100 ) ;
```

3 Now insert instructions to paint a pattern-filled rectangle

```
var image = new Image() ; image.src = "options.png" ;
var pattern = ctx.createPattern( image, "repeat" ) ;
ctx.fillStyle = pattern ; ctx.fillRect( 440, 10, 100, 100 ) ;
```

options.html

4 Save the script alongside a HTML document that incorporates this script and creates a canvas with the id value of "canvas" (just like the one listed on page 163)

5 Open the web page in your browser to see the fill options

options.png 32px x 32px

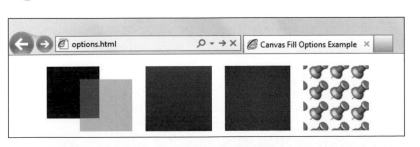

Writing text

Text can be written on an HTML5 canvas using the context object's **fillText()** and/or **strokeText()** methods. These each require three arguments to specify the text to be written, enclosed within quote marks, and the XY coordinates at which to place the bottom left corner of the text on the canvas. The text will appear painted in the canvas object's current **fillStyle** and/or **strokeStyle**.

The font in which to write the text can first be specified to the context object's **font** property. This accepts values in the same serial format as the CSS font shorthand property – to specify the font style, weight, size, and family. For example, the instruction **ctx.font = "italic bold 90px Fantasy"** specifies an italic style, bold weight, 90-pixel size, and the "Fantasy" font family. Optionally each value may be omitted from the series, so to simply specify an italic font style the instruction could read **ctx.font="italic"**.

The context object can add shadow effects to any shape it paints but is particularly useful to add drop-shadow effects to text. Shadow color, offset, and blur, are specified by the context object's **shadowColor, shadowOffsetX, shadowOffsetY**, and **shadowBlur** properties. Positive **shadowOffsetX** values position the shadow to the right of the text, and positive **shadowOffsetY** values position the shadow below the text. Negative values may be specified to position the shadow to the left and above the text respectively:

1 Create a script with a function to paint some bold text
```
function init()
{
  var canvas = document.getElementById( "canvas" ) ;
  if ( canvas.getContext )
  {
    var ctx = canvas.getContext( "2d" ) ;
    ctx.font = "bold 70px Arial, sans-serif" ;
    ctx.fillStyle = "#F30" ;
    ctx.fillText( "HTML5", 10, 60 ) ;
    /*  More instructions go here */
  }
}
onload = init ;
```

2 Next insert instructions to paint some regular text
```
ctx.font = "32px Arial" ;
ctx.fillStyle = "#09F" ;
ctx.fillText( "with Context 2D", 10, 130 ) ;
```

170

JS

write.js

...cont'd

3   Now insert instructions to paint outlined text
```
ctx.font = "italic bold 60px Fantasy" ;
ctx.strokeStyle = "#3C0" ;
ctx.strokeText( "Canvas Fun", 10, 100 ) ;
```

4   Specify values to each context object shadow property
```
ctx.shadowOffsetX = 2 ;
ctx.shadowOffsetY = 2 ;
ctx.shadowBlur = 3 ;
ctx.shadowColor = "black" ;
```

5   Finally insert instructions to paint text that will receive a drop-shadow effect
```
ctx.font = "italic bold 90px Fantasy" ;
ctx.fillStyle = "#FF0" ;
ctx.fillText( "Drop", 310, 60 ) ;
ctx.fillText( "Shadow", 310, 130 ) ;
```

6   Save the script alongside a HTML document that incorporates this script and creates a canvas with the id value of "canvas" (just like the one listed on page 163)

write.html

7   Open the web page in your browser to see the text written on the canvas and admire the drop-shadow effect

Shadow properties are global, so once values have been specified to them all further shapes painted onto the canvas will automatically receive a shadow. This can be prevented, however, by assigning a value of "transparent" to the **shadowColor** property.

Drawing lines

Lines are initially created as paths that start with the context object's **beginPath()** method, then use its **moveTo()** and **lineTo()** methods to specify the coordinates on the HTML5 canvas at which to draw the line. A call to the context object's **stroke()** method draws the line using the current **strokeStyle** and **lineWidth**.

By default the ends of the line are drawn flat, exactly abutting the canvas coordinates, but alternate line endings can be specified to the context object's **lineCap** property. Specifying a "round" value adds a semi-circular cap onto the line endings, and specifying a "square" value adds a rectangular cap. Each cap adds half the line's width. Normal line endings can be resumed by specifying the default "butt" value to the context object's **lineCap** property.

Where two lines join at an angle they will, by default, automatically receive an extension beyond the specified coordinates to create a mitered point. This extends the outer edge of each line until they meet, then fills the triangle formed by the extension. When two lines join at a very acute angle the extension needed to form the miter triangle can be lengthy, so the context object provides a **miterLimit** property to constrain the extension length. Initially this property has a value of "10", which is generally desirable, but its value can be changed if necessary.

The extended miter normally created where two lines join can be prevented by specifing a "bevel" value to the context object's **lineJoin** property, or an attractive filled arc can be added to the line ends by specifying a "round" value. Normal line joints can be resumed by specifying the default "miter" value to the context object's **lineJoin** property.

lines.js

1 Create a script with a function to paint a triangle

```
function init()
{
  var canvas = document.getElementById( "canvas" ) ;
  if ( canvas.getContext )
  {
    var ctx = canvas.getContext("2d") ; ctx.lineWidth = 20 ;
    ctx.strokeStyle = "#F30" ; ctx.beginPath() ;
    ctx.moveTo(20,130) ; ctx.lineTo(70,30) ; ctx.lineTo(120,130) ;
    ctx.closePath() ; ctx.stroke() ;
    /*  More instructions go here */
  }
}
onload = init ;
```

...cont'd

2 Next insert instructions to paint lines with different ends

```
ctx.strokeStyle = "#3C0" ;
ctx.beginPath();
ctx.lineCap = "butt" ;
ctx.moveTo( 160, 30 ) ; ctx.lineTo( 160, 120 ) ;
ctx.stroke() ;
ctx.beginPath() ;
ctx.lineCap = "round" ;
ctx.moveTo( 200, 30 ) ; ctx.lineTo( 200, 120 ) ;
ctx.stroke() ;
ctx.beginPath() ;
ctx.lineCap = "square" ;
ctx.moveTo( 240, 30 ) ; ctx.lineTo( 240, 120 ) ;
ctx.stroke() ;
```

Don't forget

Lines are painted by stroking, but when **closePath()** has been used, to create a shape, that shape can be filled.

3 Now insert instructions to paint lines with different joints

```
ctx.strokeStyle = "#09F" ;
ctx.beginPath() ;
ctx.lineJoin = "miter" ;
ctx.moveTo(280,80) ; ctx.lineTo(330,30) ; ctx.lineTo(330,120) ;
ctx.stroke() ;
ctx.beginPath() ;
ctx.lineJoin = "round" ;
ctx.moveTo(370,80) ; ctx.lineTo(420,30) ; ctx.lineTo(420,120) ;
ctx.stroke() ;
ctx.beginPath() ;
ctx.lineJoin = "bevel" ;
ctx.moveTo(460,80) ; ctx.lineTo(510,30) ; ctx.lineTo(510,120) ;
ctx.stroke() ;
```

4 Save the script alongside a HTML document that incorporates this script and creates a canvas with the id value of "canvas" (just like the one listed on page 163)

```
<!..
HTML
```
lines.html

5 Open the web page in your browser to see the lines painted on the canvas and admire their ends and joints

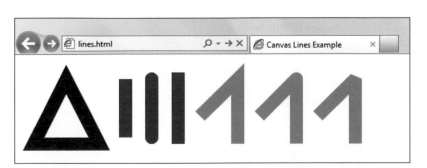

Swerving curves

The context object's **arc()** method, which was used in a previous example to paint a complete circle, can be used to paint a curved line on the canvas that is simply part of a circle's circumference. Recall that the **arc()** method requires six arguments to specify the circle's center point, radius, start angle (in radians), end angle (in radians), and the direction in which to paint – with this syntax:

ctx.arc (x, y, radius, startAngle, endAngle, direction) ;

When painting a complete circle the boolean direction value is irrelevant, but it is important when painting an arc to determine which part of the circumference is to be painted. For example, when the start angle is at 3 o'clock (zero) and the end angle is at 12 o'clock (**Math.PI/180*270**) painting counterclockwise (**true**) creates an arc that is only one quarter of the circumference, but clockwise (**false**) creates an arc of the other three quarters.

Simple curved lines that are not arcs can be painted on the canvas using the context object's **quadraticCurveTo()** method. This requires four arguments – specifying the XY coordinates of <u>one</u> invisible control point, then the XY coordinates at which the line will end. Similarly, complex curved lines can be painted on the canvas using the context object's **bezierCurveTo()** method. This requires six arguments – specifying the XY coordinates of <u>two</u> invisible control points, then the XY coordinates at which the line will end. In each case the line gets painted from the current position in the path and swerves towards the control points to create the curve:

Hot tip

The formula to convert degrees to radians is described on page 164.

curves.js

1 Create a script with a function to paint two 100-pixel square rectangles – upon which to paint arcs

```
function init()
{
  var canvas = document.getElementById( "canvas" ) ;
  if ( canvas.getContext )
  {
    var ctx = canvas.getContext( "2d" ) ;
    ctx.lineWidth = 15 ;
    ctx.strokeStyle = "#F30" ;
    ctx.fillStyle = "#FF0" ;
    ctx.fillRect( 70, 20, 100, 100 ) ;
    ctx.fillRect( 200, 20, 100, 100 ) ;
    /*  More instructions go here */
  }
}
onload = init ;
```

...cont'd

2 Next insert instructions to paint two arcs from the same circumference position, but painted in different directions
```
ctx.beginPath();
ctx.arc( 70, 70, 50, 0, Math.PI/180*90, true ) ;
ctx.stroke() ;
ctx.beginPath() ;
ctx.arc( 120, 70, 50, 0, Math.PI/180*90, false ) ;
ctx.stroke() ;
```

3 Now insert instructions to paint a filled semi-circle
```
ctx.beginPath() ;
ctx.arc( 250, 70, 50, Math.PI/180*90, Math.PI/180*270, true ) ;
ctx.fillStyle = "#3C0" ;
ctx.fill() ;
```

4 Paint a simple curve using one control point
```
ctx.strokeStyle = "#09F" ;
ctx.beginPath() ;
ctx.moveTo( 350, 10 ) ;
ctx.quadraticCurveTo( 350, 100, 440, 100 ) ;
ctx.stroke() ;
```

5 Now paint a complex curve using two control points
```
ctx.beginPath() ;
ctx.moveTo( 450, 10 ) ;
ctx.bezierCurveTo( 550, 10, 450, 100, 550, 100 ) ;
ctx.stroke() ;
```

6 Save the script alongside a HTML document that incorporates this script and creates a canvas with the id value of "canvas" (just like the one listed on page 163)

7 Open the web page in your browser to see the rectangles, arcs, and curves painted on the canvas

Don't forget

The background rectangles in this example are included to illustrate positioning – paint 1pixel square rectangles at the control point coordinates (350,100), (550,10), and (450,100) to see how they swerve the curves.

curves.html

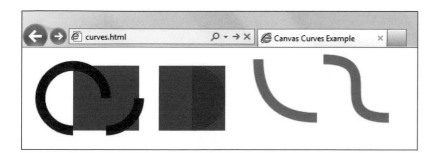

Translating coordinates

The canvas XY coordinate origin, which by default sets 0,0 at the top left corner of the canvas, can be changed by specifying new XY coordinate origins to the context object's **translate()** method. After painting at the new coordinates the canvas state can then be saved using the context object's **save()** method before restoring the initial default origin using the context object's **restore()** method. This technique is especially useful when painting multiple shapes from a script loop to move the canvas on each iteration.

Script loops can also scale shapes on successive iterations using the context object's **scale()** method. This requires two arguments to specify the "scale factor" in the horizontal and vertical directions. For example, **ctx.scale(0.5, 0.5)** scales down by 50% in each direction and **ctx.scale(1.5, 1.5)** scales up by 50%.

The context object also provides a **rotate()** method that allows the canvas to be rotated clockwise by the angle (expressed in radians) specified as its single argument. For example, specifying an argument of **Math.Pi*2/36** rotates the canvas ten degrees (360/36). Script loops can call the context object's **rotate()** method on successive iterations of a loop to paint shapes in a circular pattern:

Don't forget

The formula to convert degrees to radians is described on page 164.

translate.js

1 Create a script with a function to paint a series of square rectangles – by translating the XY canvas origin on each iteration of a loop

```
function init()
{
  var canvas = document.getElementById( "canvas" ) ;
  if ( canvas.getContext )
  {
    var i, j, ctx = canvas.getContext( "2d" ) ;
    ctx.fillStyle = "#F30" ;
    for( i = 0 ; i < 3 ; i++ )
    {
      for( j = 0 ; j < 3 ; j++ )
      {
        ctx.save() ;
        ctx.translate( 50*j, 50*i ) ;
        ctx.fillRect( 0, 0, 30, 30 ) ;
        ctx.restore() ;
      }
    }
    /*  More instructions go here */
  }
}
onload = init ;
```

2 Next insert a loop construct to paint a series of rectangles – by translating the XY canvas origin and scaling down on each iteration of the loop

```
ctx.fillStyle = "#3C0" ;
ctx.translate( 150, 0 ) ;
for( i = 0 ; i < 3 ; i++ )
{
  ctx.fillRect( 0, 0, 100, 100 ) ;
  ctx.translate( 110, 0 ) ;
  ctx.scale( 0.75, 0.75 ) ;
}
```

3 Now insert instructions to paint a series of circles – by rotating the canvas on each iteration of a loop

```
ctx.fillStyle = "#09F" ;
ctx.translate( 180, 120 ) ;
for ( i = 1 ; i < 6 ; i++ )
{
  for ( j = 0 ; j < i*6 ; j++ )
  {
    ctx.rotate( Math.PI*2 / ( i*6 ) ) ;
    ctx.beginPath() ;
    ctx.arc( 0, i*22.5, 8, 0, Math.PI*2, true ) ;
    ctx.fill() ;
  }
}
```

4 Save the script alongside a HTML document that incorporates this script and creates a canvas with the id value of "canvas" (just like the one listed on page 163)

5 Open the web page in your browser to see the shapes painted at the various coordinates by the loops

The context accumulates calls to **translate()**, **scale()**, and **rotate()** in a matrix – so after rotating, say 45 degrees, a subsequent call to **translate()** along the X axis will move diagonally, not horizontally! The next example shows how to avoid this by resetting the matrix.

translate.html

177

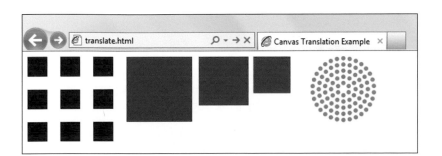

Transforming shapes

When creating shapes and paths the context object applies a "transformation matrix" to the canvas coordinates. Initially this provides an "identity transform" for the context object's methods. For example, it ensures rectangle corner angles are all 90 degrees.

The transformation matrix can be manipulated, however, to allow the context object's methods to behave differently. For example, to create skewed rectangles that do not have 90 degree corners.

Calling a context object's **transform()** method can apply a transformation by multiplying the current matrix values. For example, the call **ctx.transform(1, -0.3, 0, 1, 0, 0)** will skew rectangles when painting. The current matrix retains previous transformations but usefully can be reset to the default identity matrix with the call **ctx.setTransform(1, 0, 0, 1, 0, 0)** – so previous calls to **rotate()**, **scale()**, **translate()**, and **transform()** are forgotten.

The appearance of shapes can be also be modified by first defining a clipping path to act as a mask. Subsequently only shapes, or parts of shapes, that are inside the clipping path will be painted.

A clipping path is simply a specified path, created like any other path, that ends with a call to the context object's **clip()** method:

transform.js

1 Create a script with a function to paint a 100-pixel square rectangle – using the identity transformation matrix

```
function init()
{
  var canvas = document.getElementById( "canvas" ) ;
  if ( canvas.getContext )
  {
    var ctx = canvas.getContext( "2d" ) ;
    ctx.fillStyle = "#F30" ;
    ctx.fillRect( 20, 40, 100, 100 ) ;
    /*  More instructions go here */
  }
}
onload = init ;
```

2 Next insert instructions to paint a 100-pixel square rectangle – by multiplying the current matrix values

```
ctx.fillStyle = "#3C0" ;
ctx.transform( 1, -0.3, 0, 1, 0, 0 ) ;
ctx.fillRect( 160, 90, 100, 100 ) ;
```

3 Now insert an instruction to reset to the default identity transformation matrix – forgetting the last transformation
ctx.setTransform(1, 0, 0, 1, 0, 0) ;

4 Paint another rectangle – once more using the identity transformation matrix
ctx.fillStyle = "#09F" ;
ctx.fillRect(350, 10, 130, 130) ;

Consider each canvas element to have, by default, a clipping path that is the same size as the entire canvas – so no clipping occurs.

5 Next create a circular clipping path, centered in the rectangle just painted
ctx.beginPath() ;
ctx.arc(415, 75, 50, 0, Math.PI*2, true) ;
ctx.clip() ;

6 Now paint two more rectangles over the clipping path
ctx.fillStyle = "#FF0" ;
ctx.fillRect(350, 10, 130, 130) ;
ctx.fillStyle = "#F0F" ;
ctx.fillRect(350, 10, 65, 65) ;

7 Save the script alongside a HTML document that incorporates this script and creates a canvas with the id value of "canvas" (just like the one listed on page 163)

transform.html

8 Open the web page in your browser to see the skewed rectangle, painted using the modified transformation matrix, and the rectangles clipped by the mask

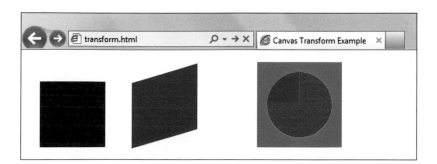

Animating the canvas

Animations can easily be created on a canvas simply by repeatedly clearing the current canvas then repainting it with shapes at a modified position. A canvas can be repainted faster than the human eye can detect so animations appear to be very smooth. The fundamental components of a canvas animation script are:

● Initialize a context object and shape starting positions

● Clear the canvas, then paint shapes onto the canvas

● Calculate new shape positions for the next repaint

Where the canvas animation has a static background and border these can be created as styles so they need not be repeatedly painted onto the canvas:

animate.js

1 Create a script that begins by declaring global variables for the context object, canvas size, XY coordinates, and direction step size
var ctx, w, h, x, y, dx, dy ;

2 Add a function that initializes a context object property and applies styles as soon as the HTML document loads

```
function init()
{
  var canvas = document.getElementById( "canvas" ) ;
  if ( canvas.getContext )
  {
    ctx = canvas.getContext( "2d" ) ;
    ctx.fillStyle = "#F30" ;
    canvas.style.background = "#FF0" ;
    canvas.style.border = "6px solid #09F" ;
    /*  More instructions go here */
  }
}
onload = init ;
```

3 Now insert instructions to initialize the global variables with XY coordinates for the starting position of a "ball", its direction step size, and canvas size

```
x = 5 ; y = 44 ;
dx = 5 ; dy = 5 ;
w = canvas.width ;
h = canvas.height ;
```

4 Insert an instruction to call a function that will calculate new XY coordinates every 25 milliseconds
setInterval(position, 25) ;

5 Next add the function that calculates new XY coordinates and stores them in global variables – after it first calls a function to actually paint the ball onto the canvas

```
function position()
{
  paint() ;
  if ( ( x+dx > w ) || ( x+dx < 0 ) ) dx = -dx ;
  if ( ( y+dy > h ) || ( y+dy < 0 ) ) dy = -dy ;
  x += dx ;
  y += dy ;
}
```

Hot tip

Notice how the polarity of the direction step gets reversed when the ball collides with a perimeter – so it doesn't bounce right off the canvas.

6 Now add the function that clears the canvas and actually paints the ball at the current stored XY coordinates

```
function paint( )
{
  ctx.clearRect( 0, 0, w, h ) ;
  ctx.beginPath() ;
  ctx.arc( x, y, 30, 0, Math.PI * 2, true ) ;
  ctx.fill() ;
}
```

181

7 Save the script alongside a HTML document that incorporates this script and creates a canvas with the id value of "canvas" (just like the one listed on page 163)

animate.html

8 Open the web page in your browser to see the animated ball bouncing around the canvas

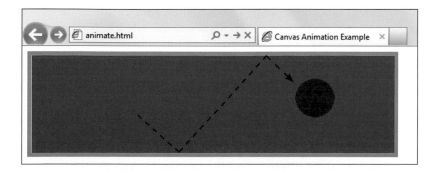

Summary

- The HTML5 **<canvas>** element creates a bitmap canvas area on a page in which script can paint shapes and text – using the canvas context object's methods and properties

- A context object's **fillStyle, strokeStyle,** and **lineWidth** properties specify the current fill color, stroke color, and line width

- A rectangle can be simply painted using the context object's **fillRect()** or **strokeRect()** methods to specify position and size

- Creating a path always begins by calling the context object's **beginPath()** method, and may be closed with **closePath()**

- A path may use the context object's **moveTo(), lineTo(),** and **arc()** methods to describe path coordinates, then paint the path on the canvas by calling its **fill()** or **stroke()** methods

- Fills may also be semi-transparent colors, gradients, or patterns

- Text painted onto a canvas by the context object's **fillText()** and **strokeText()** methods can be enhanced by a shadow effect

- A path can specify the appearance of line endings and line joints to the context object's **lineCap** and **lineJoin** properties

- A context object's **quadraticCurveTo()** and **bezierCurveTo()** methods both specify end point XY coordinates and control point XY coordinates to define curves

- The context object's **translate()** method changes the canvas XY origin, its **rotate()** method rotates the canvas, and its **scale()** method modifies a shape by a specified scale factor

- Canvas state can be saved by the context object's **save()** method and the default XY origin restored by its **restore()** method

- The context object's **transform(), setTransform(),** and **clip()** methods can be used to modify its painting behavior

- Canvas animation is achieved by repeatedly clearing the canvas and repainting it faster than the human eye can detect

10 Performing web magic

This chapter demonstrates how a document can incorporate some powerful features of HTML5 and its associated web technologies.

Creating vector graphics

Web browsers that support HTML5 also support Scalable Vector Graphics (SVG). This allows vector graphics, which can be scaled up or down any without loss of quality, to appear on web pages.

The SVG specification defines a text-based file format that provides elements and attributes to describe 2-dimensional graphics. SVG is a subset of the text-based eXtensible Markup Language (XML) so vector graphics can be created and edited in any plain text editor, or visually using a specialized graphics editor program such as Adobe Illustrator.

Static SVG images can be included in an HTML document simply by assigning their file name to an **<img>** tag's **src** attribute, and specifying the desired size to its **width** and **height** attributes.

SVG images may also be included in an HTML document by assigning their file name to an **<embed>** tag's **src** attribute, the desired size to its **width** and **height** attributes, and specifying the MIME type of "image/svg+xml" to its **type** attribute. Excitingly this exposes the elements and attributes of the vector graphic to the browser's Document Object Model (DOM) – so the image can be made dynamically interactive or animated by scripting.

Each SVG document begins with an XML document declaration:
<?xml version="1.0" encoding="UTF-8" ?>

Next follows root **<svg> </svg>** tags that will contain all other elements. The opening **<svg>** tag should have a **version** attribute, specifying the value "1.1", and an **xmlns** namespace attribute specifying the value "http://www.w3.org/2000/svg". The image size can then be specified to **width** and **height** attributes as a numerical pixel value. For cross-browser scalability, images that are to be included in HTML5 documents can specify "100%" to the **width** and **height** attributes and the image size be specified instead as XY coordinates, width, and height, to a **viewBox** attribute. For example **viewBox="0 0 550 150"**. Additionally the value "none" should be explicitly specified to a **preserveAspectRatio** attribute.

SVG components have similarities to Canvas components as they describe the image using XY coordinates, fills, and strokes, but do so to element attributes. Simple shapes can be created using SVG **<rect>** and **<circle>** elements. More elaborate shapes can be created by specifying a series of XY coordinates to the **points** attribute in **<polygon>** and **<polyline>** elements.

SVG is not a part of the HTML5 specification. Find details online at **www.w3.org/TR/SVG**.

Don't forget

Including SVG "in-line" within an HTML5 document is a hack that should be avoided – only directly include HTML then embed stylesheets, scripts, and SVG images.

...cont'd

1 Start an SVG document with the XML declaration and the root element – defining a scalable image of 550 x 150

```
<?xml version = "1.0" encoding = "UTF-8" ?>
<svg xmlns = "http://www.w3.org/2000/svg"
   version = "1.1" width = "100%" height = "100%"
   viewBox = "0 0 550 150" preserveAspectRatio="none" >
<!-- Elements go here -->
</svg>
```

vectors.svg

2 Between the root element tags, insert an element creating a square, positioning its top left corner XY coordinates

```
<rect x = "20" y = "20" width = "100" height = "100"
   fill = "#F30" stroke = "#F90" stroke-width = "6" />
```

XML, and therefore SVG, is case-sensitive (note the uppercase **B** in **viewBox**) and requires all single tags to be "self-closed" – ending as "/>".

3 Next insert an element creating a 50-pixel radius circle, positioning its center XY coordinates

```
<circle cx = "210" cy = "70" r = "50"
   fill = "#FF0" stroke = "#008000" stroke-width = "6" />
```

4 Now insert elements creating a triangle and a line following specified XY coordinates

```
<polygon points = "290,120 340,20 390,120"
   fill = "#09F" stroke = "#00F" stroke-width = "6" />

<polyline fill="none" points="430,20 430,120 530,120 530,20
440,20 480,70 520,30" stroke= "#000" stroke-width= "6" />
```

5 Now create an HTML5 document that includes an element in its body section to embed the scalable graphic

```
<embed src = "vectors.svg" type = "image/svg+xml"
   width = "550" height = "150" >
```

vectors.html

6 Save the HTML and SVG documents then open the web page in your browser to see the vector graphic shapes

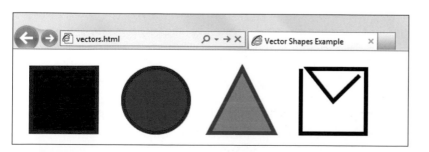

You can edit the **width** and **height** attribute values in the HTML **<img>** tag to scale the vector graphic.

Applying vector options

As with Canvas graphics, SVG images can specify fill and stroke colors using recognized color names, such as "red", hexadecimal values, such as "#FF0000" or its shorthand equivalent "#F00", or **rgb()** expressions, such as **rgb(255, 0, 0)**. The fill and stroke transparency can also be specified, within the range 0.0-1.0, to **fill-opacity** and **stroke-opacity** attributes.

In SVG a gradient fill can be defined using **<linearGradient>** or **<radialGradient>** elements, naming the gradient to an **id** attribute. These elements both require opening and closing tags to enclose **<stop>** elements, which specify a color to a **stop-color** attribute and a gradient position in the range 0.0-1.0 to an **offset** attribute. Once defined, a gradient fill can then be applied by stating its **id** name in a **url()** expression to the **fill** or **stroke** attribute of a shape. For example, **fill = "url(#MyGradient)"**.

SVG provides a **<path>** element that specifies a series of XY coordinates to a **d** (data) attribute. The coordinates can be prefixed by a single letter to indicate the type of command. For example, **d="M100,100 L100,200"** are "Move To" and "Line To" commands. Uppercase letters are absolute coordinates and lowercase are relative:

Letter:	Coordinates:	Command:
M or **m**	X,Y	Move To XY
L or **l**	X,Y	Line To XY
H or **h**	X	Horizontal Line To X
V or **v**	Y	Vertical Line To Y
Z or **z**	(none)	Close Path
C or **c**	x1,y1 x2,y2 X,Y	Curve To XY
Q or **q**	x1,y1 X,Y	Quadratic Curve To XY

Transformations can be applied in SVG by first enclosing a shape element within **<g> </g>** "grouping" tags. The opening **<g>** tag can then include a **transform** attribute to specify the type of transformation to perform. The XY coordinate origin can be changed by **translate(x, y)**, the shape's size changed by **scale(xFactor, yFactor)**, and the shape's attitude changed by **rotate(degrees)**, skewX(degrees), and skewY(degrees). Multiple transformations can be performed by nesting **<g>** elements:

Like HTML documents, SVG documents can also be validated by the W3C's online validator tool at **validator.w3.org**.

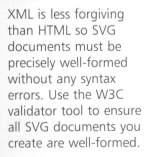

Beware

XML is less forgiving than HTML so SVG documents must be precisely well-formed without any syntax errors. Use the W3C validator tool to ensure all SVG documents you create are well-formed.

...cont'd

1 Start an SVG document with the XML declaration and the root element – exactly like those in the previous example

apply.svg

2 Between the root element tags, insert elements creating a solid rectangle and an overlapping semi-transparent one

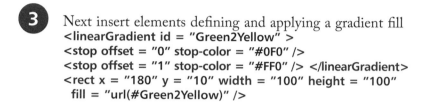

```
<rect x="20" y="10" width="80" height="80" fill="#F30"/>
<rect x = "70" y = "30" width = "80" height = "80"
  fill = "#FF0" fill-opacity = "0.7" stroke-width = "10"
  stroke = "#09F" stroke-opacity = "0.5" />
```

Hot tip

Specify a fill value of "none" when creating curves – so the browser does not close the path between the curve's end points and fill with color.

3 Next insert elements defining and applying a gradient fill

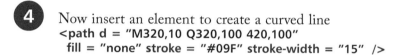

```
<linearGradient id = "Green2Yellow" >
<stop offset = "0" stop-color = "#0F0" />
<stop offset = "1" stop-color = "#FF0" /> </linearGradient>
<rect x = "180" y = "10" width = "100" height = "100"
  fill = "url(#Green2Yellow)" />
```

4 Now insert an element to create a curved line

```
<path d = "M320,10 Q320,100 420,100"
  fill = "none" stroke = "#09F" stroke-width = "15"  />
```

Don't forget

The SVG stroke is created just like that in Canvas – half on each side of the fill perimeter.

5 Insert elements to apply transformations to a rectangle

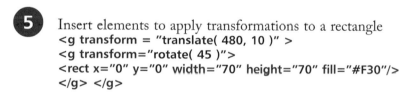

```
<g transform = "translate( 480, 10 )" >
<g transform="rotate( 45 )">
<rect x="0" y="0" width="70" height="70" fill="#F30"/>
</g> </g>
```

6 Now create an HTML5 document that includes an element in its body section to embed the scalable graphic

```
<embed src = "apply.svg" type = "image/svg+xml"
  width = "550" height = "150" >
```

apply.html

7 Save the HTML and SVG documents then open the web page in your browser to see the applied vector options

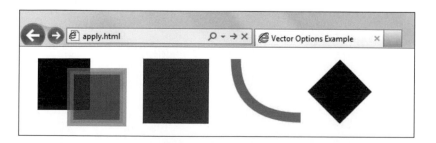

Employing a vector editor

Simple vector graphics can be easily created in any plain text editor, as demonstrated by the previous two examples, but vector graphics incorporating anything more than the simplest of shapes are best created by employing a visual vector graphic editor.

The industry standard vector graphic editor is the excellent Adobe Illustrator product. Other popular choices include the Inkscape vector graphic editor, which unlike Illustrator is available for free, and the Serif DrawPlus editor – whose Starter Edition is free.

Visual vector graphic editors contain similar tools to draw shapes, with fill and stroke properties, and allow the graphic to be saved in a variety of file formats. Saving as a Scalable Vector Graphic typically produces a standalone graphic that can be directly opened full size by any web browser that supports HTML5. As SVG is text-based the resulting file can be edited for cross-browser scalability for inclusion in web pages:

Hot tip

Inkscape can be found online at **inkscape.org** and the Serif DrawPlus Starter edition is at **www.serif.com/drawplus/FreeDownloads**.

editor.svg

1 Launch a visual vector graphic editor and use the tools to create a graphic – Serif DrawPlus has a clip art gallery of ready graphics that can be dragged onto the drawing area

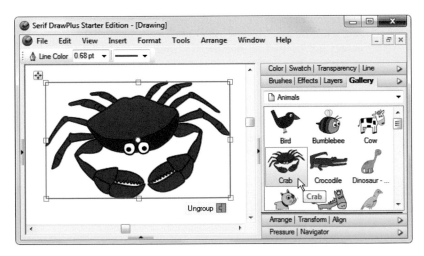

2 Prepare to export the graphic by grouping together all the shapes into a single object and ensure that the object is "selected", typically indicated by a highlighted border – this should set the object border as the graphic size rather than the border of the entire drawing area

3 Choose the appropriate File menu option to Save or Export the graphic from the editor menu and select Scalable Vector Graphics as the file format

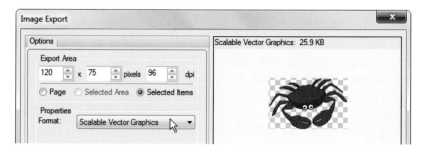

4 Next open the resulting SVG file in a plain text editor and edit the opening root element tag
```
<svg xmlns = "http://www.w3.org/2000/svg"
  version = "1.1" width = "100%" height = "100%"
  viewBox = "0 0 120 75" preserveAspectRatio = "none" >
```

5 Now create an HTML5 document that includes two elements in its body section to display the scalable vector graphic – one at its original size, and one scaled up without preserving the aspect ratio
```
<img src = "editor.svg" width = "120" height = "75" >
<!-- Now scale width x 3.5 and height x 2 -->
<img src = "editor.svg" width = "400" height = "150" >
```

editor.html

6 Save the HTML and SVG documents then open the web page in any browser that supports HTML5 to see the vector graphic in its original and scaled up forms

Interacting with vectors

SVG graphics embedded in an HTML5 document maintain an XML Document Object Model (DOM) node tree of all their elements and attributes. This is separate from the HTML DOM but can be easily accessed through scripting to allow the HTML document to interact with the embedded SVG graphic.

The key to accessing the embedded XML DOM is to first create a reference object to the SVG document with a **getSVGDocument()** method. Then elements, attributes, and text in the SVG document can be addressed via the reference object:

interact.html

  Create an HTML5 document that incorporates a script, embeds an SVG graphic, and includes a text input field and a push button in its body section

```
<script src = "interact.js" > </script>

<embed id = "svgDoc" src = "interact.svg"
  type = "image/svg+xml" width = "550" height = "70" >
<br> <input id = "htmTxt" >
<button id= "htmBtn">Send To SVG Document</button>
```

interact.svg

2 Next create the SVG graphic containing text and a circle

```
<?xml version = "1.0" encoding = "UTF-8" ?>
<svg xmlns = "http://www.w3.org/2000/svg"
  version = "1.1" width = "100%" height = "100%"
  viewBox = "0 0 550 70" preserveAspectRatio = "none" >

<text id="svgTxt" x="10" y="50" font-size="30"  fill="#F30"
  font-family="Comic Sans MS" >SVG Text</text>

<circle id = "svgBtn" cx = "460" cy = "40" r = "30"
  fill = "#F30" cursor = "pointer" /> </svg>
```

interact.js

3 Now begin a script that creates a reference to the SVG document and elements within both documents (as global variables) when the documents have loaded

```
var svgDoc, svgTxt, svgBtn, htmTxt ;
function init()
{
  svgDoc =
  document.getElementById("svgDoc").getSVGDocument() ;
  svgTxt = svgDoc.getElementById( "svgTxt" ) ;
  svgBtn = svgDoc.getElementById( "svgBtn" ) ;
  htmTxt = document.getElementById( "htmTxt" ) ;
  /* More instructions go here */
} onload = init ;
```

4 Insert instructions to specify click event-handler functions for the HTML push button and the SVG circle
svgDoc.getElementById("svgBtn").onclick = send2htm ;
document.getElementById("htmBtn").onclick = send2svg;

5 Next add both event-handler functions to the script
```
function send2svg() {
   svgTxt.lastChild.replaceWholeText( htmTxt.value ) ;
   htmTxt.value = "" ;
}

function send2htm() {
   htmTxt.value = svgTxt.lastChild.wholeText ;
   svgTxt.lastChild.replaceWholeText( "SVG Text" );
}
```

Hot tip

Notice that in the SVG (XML) DOM the actual text is contained in the **wholeText** property of the **lastChild** node of the SVG **<text>** element.

6 Save all three documents then open the web page in your browser and enter some text – click the button and circle to see your text move from HTML to SVG and back

191

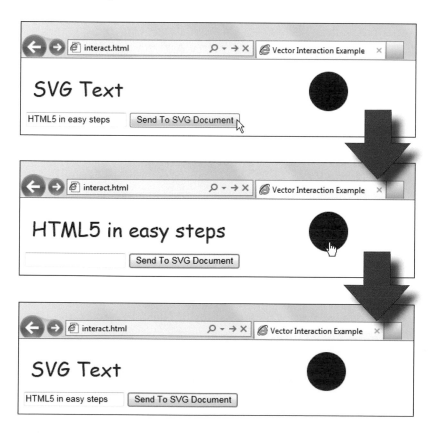

Don't forget

This example, and all further examples in this book, are served via the HTTP protocol from a web server (not from a local file system) — this allows the browser to confirm all files originate from the same domain if it's a required precaution.

Animating vector graphics

As embedded SVG graphics maintain an accessible node tree of all their elements and attributes they can be easily animated by dynamically changing element properties – possibly manipulating color, size, shape, content, or position:

animation.html

1 Create an HTML5 document that incorporates a script, and embeds an SVG graphic to be animated

```
<script src = "animation.js" > </script>
```

```
<embed id = "svgDoc" src = "animation.svg"
type = "image/svg+xml" width = "550" height = "150" >
```

animation.svg

2 Next create the SVG graphic containing a filled rectangle, a circle, and a stroked rectangle

```
<?xml version = "1.0" encoding = "UTF-8" ?>
<svg xmlns = "http://www.w3.org/2000/svg"
  version = "1.1" width = "100%" height = "100%"
  viewBox = "0 0 550 150" preserveAspectRatio = "none" >

<rect x = "3" y = "3" width = "538" height = "138"
  fill = "#FF0" stroke = "none" />

<circle id = "ball" cx = "5" cy = "44" r = "30"
  fill = "#F30" />

<rect x = "3" y = "3" width = "544" height = "144"
   fill = "none" stroke = "#09F" stroke-width = "6" />

</svg>
```

animation.js

3 Now begin a script that creates a reference to the SVG document, and a reference to the circle element within it (as a global variable) when the documents have loaded

```
var ball, w, h, x, y, dx = 5, dy = 5 ;

function init()
{
  var embed = document.getElementById( "svgDoc" ) ;
  var svgDoc =  embed.getSVGDocument() ;
  ball = svgDoc.getElementById( "ball" ) ;
  /* More instructions go here */
}
onload = init ;
```

4 Insert instructions to initialize all other global variables with values taken from the SVG elements' attributes

```
w = embed.getAttribute( "width" ) ;
h = embed.getAttribute( "height" ) ;
x = ball.getAttribute( "x" ) ;
y = ball.getAttribute( "y" ) ;
```

5 Next insert an instruction to call a function that will calculate new XY coordinates every 25 milliseconds

```
setInterval( position, 25 ) ;
```

6 Now add the function that actually moves the circle then calculates and stores the new coordinates

```
function position()
{
  ball.setAttribute( "cx", x ) ;
  ball.setAttribute( "cy", y ) ;
  if ( ( x+dx > w ) || ( x+dx < 0 ) ) dx = -dx ;
  if ( ( y+dy > h ) || ( y+dy < 0 ) ) dy = -dy ;
  x += dx ; y += dy ;
}
```

7 Save the HTML document and script then open the web page in your browser to see the animated ball bouncing around the rectangle

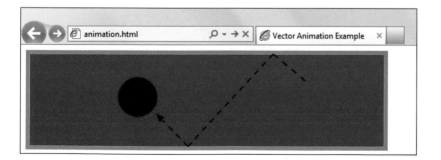

When comparing SVG to Canvas remember that SVG is document-based, draws scalable vectors, and maintains a DOM tree – so is best suited for mouse interaction. Canvas on the other hand is script-based, paints bitmaps, and does not maintain a DOM tree – but performs better when animating a large number of objects so may be best suited for keyboard interaction. The next example demonstrates one additional possibility Canvas offers.

Hot tip

The order of the shape elements is important as it allows the "ball" to slide between the border and the background when it meets the rectangle boundaries.

Don't forget

This example may seem familiar – it exactly replicates the Canvas animation example on page 181, but uses SVG animation instead.

Manipulating bitmap pixels

The amazing ability to manipulate the color of pixels in an image is provided in HTML5 by the Canvas2D API, which was introduced in the previous chapter. The canvas context object has a **drawImage()** method that can copy a specified image onto a canvas, at specified XY coordinates. Information describing the color of each pixel on the canvas can then be stored in a "CanvasPixelArray" using the context object's **getImageData()** method. This method requires four arguments to specify the XY coordinates, width, and height, of the area to be stored.

A CanvasPixelArray object has **width**, **height**, and **data** properties. Of most interest, the **data** property is an array of the red, green, blue, and alpha components of each pixel stored in sequence. For example, with [r1, g1, b1, a1, r2, g2, b2, a2, r3, g3, b3, a3] the array elements r1, g1, b1, a1 describe the red, greeen, blue, and alpha components of the very first pixel – giving each color a numerical value in the range 0-255. Manipulating the numerical value in the array modifies the stored image data. The modified image can then be painted back onto the canvas, using the context object's **putImageData()** method to specify the array name, and the XY coordinates on the canvas at which to paint the image:

The Canvas2D API is part of the HTML5 specifications. Find details at **dev.w3.org/ html5/canvas-api**.

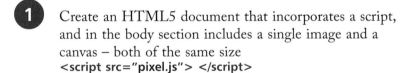

pixel.html

1 Create an HTML5 document that incorporates a script, and in the body section includes a single image and a canvas – both of the same size
```
<script src="pixel.js"> </script>

<img id="pixel" src="pixel.png"
        width="215" height="150" alt="Blue Flag" >
<canvas id="canvas" width="215" height="150" >
[Fallback Message]</canvas>
```

pixel.js

2 Now create a script to copy the image onto the canvas when the document has loaded
```
function init()
{
 var canvas = document.getElementById( "canvas" ) ;
 if ( canvas.getContext )
 {
  var ctx = canvas.getContext( "2d" ) ;
  var img = document.getElementById( "pixel" ) ;
  ctx.drawImage( img, 0, 0 ) ;
  /* More instructions go here */
 }
} onload = init ;
```

...cont'd

3 Next insert an instruction to read all pixels from the canvas into a pixel array
var pixels =
 ctx.getImageData(0, 0, img.width, img.height) ;

4 Then insert a loop construct to iterate through each RGBA alpha component of the pixel array
for (var i = 3 ; i < pixels.data.length ; i +=4)
{
 /* More instructions go here */
}

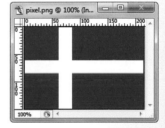

Hot tip

White has an RGB color value of 255,255,255 so the script tests each green color component for the value 255 to identify each white pixel.

5 In the loop construct, insert instructions to ignore white pixels but change all blue pixels to red
if (pixels.data[i-2] !== 255)
 {
 pixels.data[i-1] = 0 ; // Set b=0 – remove blue
 pixels.data[i-3] =255 ; // Set r=255 – make red
 }

6 Finally insert an instruction to paint the manipulated pixel array onto the canvas
ctx.putImageData(pixels, 0, 0) ;

7 Save the HTML document and script then open the web page in your browser, via a web server, to see the modified image painted onto the canvas

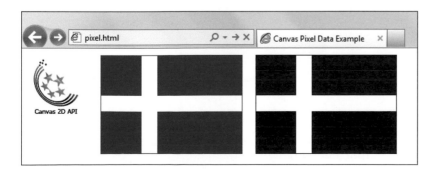

Beware

To use this technique the source image for the **drawImage()** method must be served via the HTTP protocol from a web server (not a local file system) and it must be located on the same domain as the HTML document.

Dragging & dropping objects

The ability to allow the user to drag page objects and drop them onto a target is supported in HTML5 by the DragNdrop API. This specifies many events that fire when the user drags an object but most important are the "dragstart", "dragover", and "drop" events. Event-handlers need to be scripted for each one of these events:

The DragNdrop API is part of the HTML5 specifications. For details refer to **www.w3.org**.

- **ondragstart event-handler** – to specify the Text data to be attached to the object being dragged, when dragging starts

- **ondragover event-handler** – to cancel the default behavior of the drop target, thereby allowing objects to be dropped on it

- **ondrop event-handler** – to define what should happen when an object gets dropped on the drop target

Additionally the ondrop event-handler should typically ensure that the target cannot be dropped on itself:

dragndrop.html

1 Create an HTML5 document that incorporates a script, and includes drag and drop images in the body section, along with an empty list
```
<script src="dragndrop.js"> </script>

<img id="bin" src="bin.png">
<img id="Red" src="red.png">
<img id="Yellow" src="yel.png">
<img id="Green" src="grn.png">
<fieldset><legend>Folders Dropped:</legend>
<ol id="msg" ></ol></fieldset>
```

Folders Dropped:

dragndrop.js

2 Next create a script that gets a reference for each image and the list when the HTML document has loaded
```
function init()
{
  var bin = document.getElementById( "bin" ) ;
  var gfx = document.getElementsByTagName( "img" ) ;
  var msg = document.getElementById( "msg" ) ;
  /*  More instructions go here */
}
onload = init ;
```

3 For the ondragstart event-handler, add a loop to attach the id of the image element being dragged as Text data

```
for( var i = 0 ; i < gfx.length ; i++ )
{
  gfx[ i ].ondragstart = function( event )
  { event.dataTransfer.setData( "Text", this.id ) ; } ;
}
```

4 For the ondragover event-handler, cancel the default behavior of the bin – so objects can be dropped on it

```
bin.ondragover = function( event ) { return false ; } ;
```

5 For the ondrop event-handler, first get the id of the object being dropped and a reference for that image element

```
bin.ondrop = function( event )
{
  var did = event.dataTransfer.getData( "Text" ) ;
  var tag = document.getElementById( did ) ;
  /*  More instructions go here */
} ;
```

6 Next insert an instruction to write the id of the dropped element into the list – unless it is the bin image itself

```
if( did === "bin" ) { return false ; }
else { msg.innerHTML += "<li>"+did+"</li>" ; }
```

7 Finally insert instructions to remove the dropped image element from the page and to end the drop function

```
tag.parentNode.removeChild( tag ) ;  return false ;
```

8 Save the HTML document and script then open the web page in your browser – drag'n'drop the folders on the bin

Hot tip

Notice that the arguments to the dragstart event's **dataTransfer.setData()** method specify the data format and the actual data – in this case the "Text" format and the id of the dragged element.

197

Beware

The efficiency of the DragNdrop API is the subject of some controversy so it may be subject to revision.

Storing user data

The ability to store user data is supported in HTML5 by the excellent Web Storage API that makes storing user data a breeze. This provides a **localStorage** object, which retains stored data even after the browser has been closed, and the **sessionStorage** object, which retains stored data only until the browser gets closed. Each of these objects has identical methods to store and retrieve data.

The **setItem()** method requires two arguments to specify a key and the data to be stored. For example, using the key "Name" in **localStorage.setItem("Name", "Mike")**. Stored data can then be retrieved, by specifying the key as the sole argument to the **getItem()** method, or removed by specifying the key as the sole argument to a **removeItem()** method. Additionally all stored items can be deleted using the **clear()** method – without any arguments.

The Web Storage API is part of the HTML5 specifications. Find details at **dev.w3.org/ html5/webstorage**.

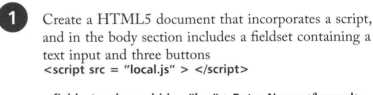

local.html

1 Create a HTML5 document that incorporates a script, and in the body section includes a fieldset containing a text input and three buttons

```
<script src = "local.js" > </script>

<fieldset><legend id = "leg" >Enter Name</legend>
<input type = "text" id = "username" >
<button onclick="storeName()">Store Name</button>
<button onclick="recallName()">Recall Name</button>
<button onclick="removeName()">Remove Name</button>
</fieldset>
```

local.js

2 Now create a script with an event-handler function for the first button – to save the user data in local storage if valid

```
function storeName()
{
  var username =
        document.getElementById("username").value ;
  if( username === "null" || username === "" ) return false;
  localStorage.setItem( "user", username ) ;
   /*  More instructions go here */
}
```

Backstroke characters in this script simply escape some quote marks.

3 Next in the script function, insert instructions to clear the text field and display a confirmation message

```
document.getElementById( "username" ).value = "" ;
document.getElementById("leg").innerHTML =
"\""+ localStorage.getItem("user") + "\" is Stored";
```

...cont'd

4 Add an event-handler function for the second button – to retrieve and display the user data in local storage

```
function recallName()
{
  if( localStorage.getItem("user") === null ) return false ;
  document.getElementById( "username" ).value = "" ;
  document.getElementById("leg").innerHTML =
  "Stored Name is \""+ localStorage.getItem("user") + "\"" ;
}
```

5 Finally add an event-handler function for the third button – to remove the user data in local storage

```
function removeName()
{
  if( localStorage.getItem("user") === null ) return false ;
  document.getElementById("leg").innerHTML =
  "\"" + localStorage.getItem("user") + "\" is Removed" ;
  localStorage.removeItem("user") ;
  document.getElementById( "username" ).value = "" ;
}
```

6 Save the HTML document and script, then open the web page in your browser and store user name data

7 Restart your browser and re-open this web page then push the "Recall Name" button to see the data has been retained – push the "Remove Name" button to delete the user data from local storage

Hot tip

A shorthand alternative lets you simply tag the key onto the object name. For example, **localStorage. setItem("A","1")** can be expressed as **localStorage.A="1"** and **localStorage.getItem("A")** as **localStorage.A**.

Beware

All data in **localStorage** and **sessionStorage** is stored as string values – so attempting to add retrieved values of 5 and 7 will get concatenated as 57, not totalled to 12.

Editing live content

The Web Storage API, introduced in the previous example, makes storing user data in HTML5 so much easier than the old method of setting "cookies". Restrictions allow only 20 cookies per domain and limit the amount of text data they can each store to 4Kb – allowing a maximum total of (20x4) 80 Kiloybytes per domain. By stark contrast Web Storage allows over 5 Megabytes per domain.

The **localStorage** object, that retains user data after the browser gets closed, is useful to store constant user data – such as user names and passwords. The **sessionStorage** object, that releases user data after the browser gets closed, is useful to store transient user data – such as the items in a shopping session basket.

The content of any page element can be made editable, so the user can modify its content, by adding a global **contenteditable** attribute to the element. The modified content can then be stored by **sessionStorage** to be temporarily available until the user closes the browser, thereby ending the session:

session.html

1 Create an HTML5 document that incorporates a script, and in the body section include an editable list and three buttons – to store and retrieve session data
<script src = "session.js" > </script>

**<ul contenteditable="true" id="list">
<li>Red<li>Green<li>Blue</ul>**

**<button id="restore" onclick="restore()">
Restore Original List</button>**

**<button id="show" onclick="show()">
Restore My List</button>**

**<button id="wipe" onclick="wipe()">
Delete My List</button>**

session.js

2 Now create a script with a function to store the original list items as soon as the HTML document has loaded
**function init()
{
  sessionStorage.setItem("originalList" ,
      document.getElementById("list".innerHTML) ;
}
onload = init ;**

...cont'd

3 Next add an event-handler function for the first button – to store the edited list, then display the original list
```
function restore() {
sessionStorage.setItem( "customList" ,
        document.getElementById( "list" ).innerHTML ) ;
document.getElementById( "list" ).innerHTML =
                sessionStorage.getItem( "originalList" ) ;
}
```

4 Now add an event-handler function for the second button – to simply display the stored edited list
```
function show() {
document.getElementById( "list" ).innerHTML =
                sessionStorage.getItem( "customList" );
}
```

5 Add an event-handler function for the third button – to display the original list, then remove the stored edited list
```
function wipe() {
document.getElementById( "list" ).innerHTML =
                sessionStorage.getItem( "originalList" ) ;
sessionStorage.removeItem( "customList" ) ;
}
```

6 Save the HTML document and script then open the web page, edit the list, and use the buttons for session storage

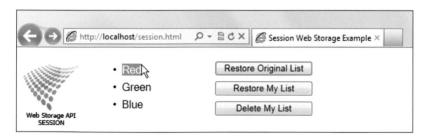

Hot tip

If you want an entire document to be editable you can simply include the script instruction **document.designMode** ="on"; (notice that's "**on**" not "**true**") in the **init()** function – much easier than adding lots of **contenteditable** attributes.

Don't forget

Items in session storage remain available even when the user navigates to a different domain then returns. They are only lost when the browser gets closed.

Cross-document messaging

The ability to allow plain text messages to be securely sent between documents is supported in HTML5 by the Messaging API. This is even possible when the documents are hosted on two different domains. For example, a document hosted on the local domain might include an inline frame containing a document from a different domain, which can securely send messages to each other.

To send a message to another document a reference to the receiving document's containing window is first required by the sending document. For an inline frame this is available from its **contentWindow** property. The Messaging API then provides it a **postMessage()** method that requires two arguments – to specify the message to be sent, and the target document domain. For example, **otherWindow.postMessage("Hello", "http://example.com")**.

In order to receive a message sent from another document a message "listener" must first be added to the receiving document. This requires three arguments be supplied to that window's **addEventListener()** method – to specify it should listen for a "message" type, the event-handler function to process the message, and a boolean **false** value to indicate no further processing is required.

The message is passed to the event-handler as an "event" that has an **origin** property, containing the domain of the sending document, and a **data** property, containing the text message.

msg-send.html

1 Create an HTML5 document that incorporates a script, a paragraph to display the document domain, an inline frame for a remote domain, and a "Send Message" button

```
<script src = "http://localhost/msg.js" > </script>
```

```
<p id = "host" >Main Page Domain: </p>
<iframe id = "ifr" width = "450" height = "120"
  src= "http://xdoc.bravehost.com/msg-receive.html" >
</iframe>
<button onclick = "sendMsg()" >Send Message</button>
```

msg-receive.html

2 Next create an HTML document that incorporates the same script and has paragraphs to display the domain and message

```
<script src = "http://localhost/msg.js" > </script>
```

```
<p id = "host">Iframe Page Domain: </p>
<p id = "para" ></p>
```

The Messaging API is part of the HTML5 specifications. Find details at **dev.w3.org/ html5/postmsg**.

3 Now create the script to send and receive a message

```
function init() {
  document.getElementById("host").innerHTML +=
                              document.domain ;
  addEventListener( "message", readMsg, false ) ;
} onload = init ;

function sendMsg() {
  var win=document.getElementById("ifr").contentWindow ;
  win.postMessage( "Message Received from: " +
  document.domain, "http://xdoc.bravehost.com" ) ;
}

function readMsg(event) {
  if ( event.origin === "http://localhost" )
  document.getElementById("para").innerHTML =
                              ( event.data ) ;
}
```

msg.js

4 Save the first HTML document and script on the local domain, and the second HTML document on the remote domain, then click to send a cross-document message

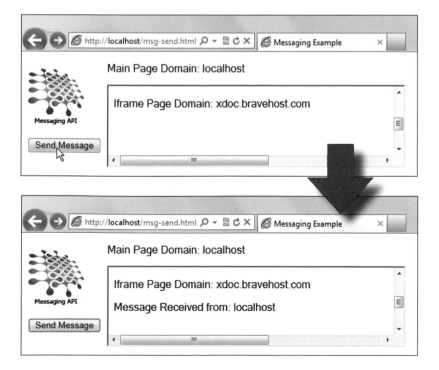

203

Pin-pointing the user

The ability to pin-point the user's geographic location is supported in HTML5 by the wonderful Geolocation API. This first requests the user's consent to share location details – to send information about nearby wireless access points and the computer's IP address to, say, Google Location Services. This service returns the user's estimated latitude and longitude coordinates. Coordinates successfully retrieved can be displayed on the page and supplied to the Google Maps service to acquire a map at that location:

geolocation.html

1 Create an HTML document that incorporates two scripts, and includes two empty paragraphs in the body section

```
<script src = "geolocation.js" > </script>
<script src =
    "http://maps.google.com/maps/api/js?sensor=false">
</script>
<p id = "msg" ></p> <p id = "map" ></p>
```

geolocation.js

2 Now create a script with a function that attempts to seek the user location when the HTML document has loaded

```
function init()
{
  if ( navigator.geolocation )
  { document.getElementById( "msg" ).innerHTML =
        "Geolocation service is trying to find you...";
    navigator.geolocation.getCurrentPosition
        ( successFunction, errorFunction ) ; }
  else { document.getElementById( "msg" ).innerHTML =
  "Your browser does not support Geolocation service" ; }
} onload = init ;
```

The Geolocation API is not strictly part of the HTML5 specification. You can find details online at **dev.w3.org/geo/api**.

3 Next add a function to display a message if the attempt fails

```
function errorFunction( position )
{  document.getElementById( "msg" ).innerHTML =
    "Geolocation service cannot find you at this time." ; }
```

4 Add a success function to display the retrieved coordinates when the attempt succeeds

```
function successFunction( position )
{
  var lat = position.coords.latitude ;
  var lng = position.coords.longitude ;
  document.getElementById( "msg" ).innerHTML =
  "Found you at...<br>Latitude: "+lat+", Longitude: "+lng ;
  /* More instructions go here */
}
```

...cont'd

5 Now in the success function, add instructions to load a map from Google Maps – using the retrieved coordinates

```
var latlng = new google.maps.LatLng( lat, lng ) ;
var options = { zoom: 18, center : latlng,
        mapTypeId: google.maps.MapTypeId.ROADMAP } ;
var map = new google.maps.Map
        ( document.getElementById( "map" ), options ) ;
var marker = new google.maps.Marker(
        { position: latlng, map: map, title:"You are here" } ) ;
```

6 Save the HTML document and script then open the web page – agree to share your location to get pin-pointed

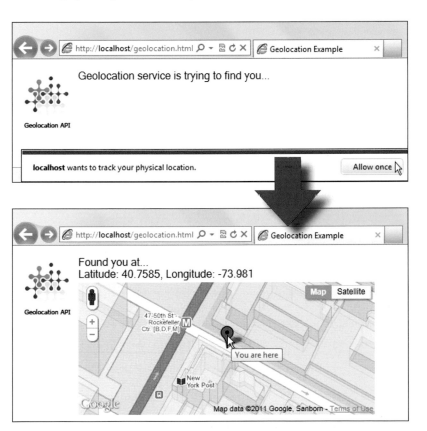

205

Scalable Vector Graphics, native Drag-and-drop capability, enhanced Web Storage for user data, secure cross-document Messaging between domains, and Geolocation services, present fantastic exciting possibilities - thanks to HTML5.

Summary

- Scalable Vector Graphics (SVG) are text-based documents describing images that can be scaled without any loss of quality

- SVG images can be included in a HTML document using the HTML **<img>** or **<embed>** elements

- Shapes are created in SVG by elements, such as the SVG **<rect>**, **<circle>**, **<polygon>**, and **<path>** elements

- The **<linearGradient>**, **<radialGradient>**, and **<stop>** elements are used to define gradient fills in SVG

- Transformations, such as **translate()**, **scale()**, or **rotate()**, can be specified to the **transform** attribute of a **<g>** grouping element

- Anything more than the simplest SVG shapes are best created by employing a visual vector graphic editor, such as Inkscape

- Embedded SVG graphics maintain a node tree of elements so can easily be made interactive or animated by scripting – after creating a reference with the **getSVGDocument()** method

- The Canvas 2D API can be used to manipulate pixel color via the **data** property of its CanvasPixelArray object

- The DragNdrop API allows the user to drag page objects and drop them onto a target within the page – by scripting **ondragstart**, **ondragover**, and **ondrop** event-handler functions

- The Web Storage API provides the ability to store user data – either permanently with its **localStorage** object, or temporarily until the browser gets closed with its **sessionStorage** object

- The Messaging API allows plain text messages to be sent securely between documents with its **postMessage()** method – and the documents need not be on the same domain

- The Geolocation API provides the ability to pin-point the user's location by estimating latitude and longitude coordinates – but only if the user consents to send information

Handy reference

This section of the book lists and describes HTML5 elements and attributes.

Global HTML5 attributes

The attributes in the table below may each be included in any HTML5 element, so are therefore known as "global" attributes.

Attribute:	Description:
accesskey	Suggests a keyboard shortcut key Example: accesskey="A"
class	Specifies one or more space-separated class names to which the element belongs Example: class="recipes fish"
contenteditable	Indicates that the element is an area in which the user may edit the content Example: contenteditable="true"
dir	Specifies the text direction with values of ltr (left-to-right) or rtl (right-to-left) Example: dir="rtl"
draggable	Indicates that the element may be dragged and dropped at another location Example: draggable="true"
id	Specifies an identity name for the element that must be unique within the document Example: id="item_22"
lang	Specifies the general content language as a short standard abbreviation Example: lang="fr" (French)
spellcheck	Suggests whether the element content can be checked for spelling Example: spellcheck="true"
style	Specifies one or more CSS style rules Example: style="border:2px solid red;"
tabindex	Specifies the element's sequential position reached by pressing the Tab key Example: tabindex="3"
title	Suggests advisory information for the element, such as a Tooltip Example: title="This item is draggable"

Hot tip

A comprehensive list of standard language abbreviations is maintained by the Internet Assigned Numbers Authority (IANA) and can be found online at **www.iana.org/ assignments/language-subtag-registry**.

...cont'd

In addition to those global attributes in the table opposite the following global attributes in the table below may also be included in any HTML5 element. These attributes each allow a specified script function to be called when a particular event occurs on the element, so are therefore known as "event-handler" attributes.

Attribute:	Description:
onabort onerror	Specifies functions to respond to the events that fire when the user aborts the download of page content or when an error occurs
onblur onfocus	Specifies functions to respond to the events that fire when the user moves focus onto and away from the element
onchange onselect	Specifies functions to respond to the events that fire when the user changes or selects the element content
onclick ondblclick onmousedown onmouseup	Specifies functions to respond to the events that fire when the user clicks or double-clicks the left mouse button
onkeydown onkeypress onkeyup	Specifies functions to respond to the events that fire when the user presses and releases a keyboard key
onload	Specifies a function to respond to the event that fires when content has loaded
onmousemove onmouseover onmouseout	Specifies functions to respond to the events that fire when the user moves the mouse pointer over the element
onsubmit	Specifies a function to respond to the event that fires when the user submits a form to the server
ondragstart ondragover ondragend ondragenter ondragleave ondrag, ondrop	Specifies functions to respond to the events that fire when the user drags or drops an element

Don't forget

Although all these attributes can be used in any HTML5 element they are not necessarily useful in all elements.

HTML5 element tags

The following tables describe HTML5 element tags together with their element-specific attributes. These attributes may be included within the associated tag in addition to the global attributes and event-handler attributes described on pages 208-209.

HTML5 tags are NOT case-sensitive so may appear as uppercase or lowercase characters.

Element:	Description:
<!-- -->	Comment tag. Encloses text comments that are ignored by the browser. Empty element – no closing tag required
Attributes:	None
<!DOCTYPE>	Document type declaration tag. The very first element in each document, defining the HTML markup version being used. Empty element – no closing tag required
Attributes:	**HTML** - Required to identify the markup version as HTML5 and so set the browser to Standards Mode
<a>	Anchor tag. Encloses a hyperlink, or acts as a placeholder
Attributes:	**href** – States the URL of a hyperlink target Or when used to specify a placeholder... **target** – Specifies a context name **hreflang** – Advises of the target language **media** – Advises of the target media **rel** – Advises of the target relationship **type** – Advises of the target MIME type
<abbr>	Abbreviation tag. Encloses an abbreviation
Attributes:	**title** – (global attribute) can be included to specify an expansion of the abbreviation
<address>	Address tag. Encloses contact information
Attributes:	None

...element tags cont'd

Element:	Description:
\<area>	Area tag. Specifies an area of an image map defined by its attributes. Empty element – no closing tag required
Attributes:	**alt** – Specifies alternative text like a tooltip **shape** – Defines the area shape **coords** – States the area's XY coordinates **href** – States the URL of a hyperlink target **target** – Specifies a context name **hreflang** – Advises of the target language **media** – Advises of the target media **rel** – Advises of the target relationship **type** – Advises of the target MIME type
\<article>	Article tag. Encloses a self-contained composition within a page
Attributes:	None
\<aside>	Aside tag. Encloses content related to the adjacent content, such as in a sidebar
Attributes:	None
\<audio>	Audio tag. Encloses source elements and specifies audio media content
Attributes:	**src** – States the URL of the audio resource **preload** – Advises of play likelihood **autoplay** – Specifies automatic play **loop** – Specifies automatic replay **controls** – Provides user interface controls
\<b>	Bold tag. Encloses content that is to be displayed in a bold font
Attributes:	None
\<base>	Base tag. Specifies a default address or a default target for all links on a page Empty element – no closing tag required
Attributes:	**href** – States the URL of a hyperlink target **target** – Specifies a context name

Beware

Web browsers support different codecs for audio playback, so it is recommended the **\<audio>** tag be used to enclose **\<source>** tags that specify alternative audio formats.

...element tags cont'd

Element:	Description:
<bdo>	Bi-Directional Override tag. Encloses text to be written in a specific direction
Attributes:	**dir** – Specifies text direction as either "rtl" (right-to-left) or "ltr" (left-to-right)
<blockquote>	Blockquote tag. Encloses a long quotation, typically automatically inset from preceding content
Attributes:	**cite** – Specifies a URL where the origin of the quotation is available
<body>	Body tag. Encloses the entire contents of the document including text, hyperlinks, images, tables, lists, audio, video, etc.
Attributes:	**onload** – (global attribute) Specifies script to run when the document has loaded **onunload** – (global attribute) Specifies script to run when the document unloads **onbeforeunload** – Specifies script to run before the document unloads **onbeforeprint**, **onafterprint** – Specifies script to run before and after preparing the document for print or print preview **onhashchange** – Specifies script to run when following a hyperlink to a target within the same document **onoffline**, **ononline** – Specifies script to run when connection is lost and restored **onmessage** – Specifies script to run when the user sends a cross-document message **onresize** – Specifies script to run when the browser window size gets changed
** **	Break tag. Inserts a single line break Empty element – no closing tag required
Attributes:	None

Don't forget

The global attributes **onblur**, **onerror**, **onfocus**, and **onload** each specify event-handlers for the top-level window object when included within the **<body>** tag.

...element tags cont'd

Element:	Description:
\<button\>	Button tag. Encloses text to appear on a user-activated button
Attributes:	**type** – Specifies whether the button has a "button","submit", or "reset" action **name**, **value** – Specifies the element's name/value key pair for form submission **disabled** – Suppresses user interaction
\<canvas\>	Canvas tag. Inserts an invisible area that can be drawn in by script
Attributes:	**width** – Specifies the area's width **height** – Specifies the area's height
\<caption\>	Caption tag. Encloses a table caption
Attributes:	None
\<cite\>	Citation tag. Encloses the title of a work, such as a book, film, or song
Attributes:	None
\<code\>	Caption tag. Encloses computer programming code text
Attributes:	None
\<col\>	Column tag. Identifies one or more table columns within a column group Empty element – no closing tag required
Attributes:	**span** – Specifies a number of columns
\<colgroup\>	Column group tag. Encloses one or more column tags, or specifies a number of columns within the group
Attributes:	**span** – Specifies the number of columns if no column tags are enclosed
\<dd\>	Definition-list Description tag. Encloses the description of a definition term within a definition list
Attributes:	None

Hot tip

The methods and properties of the Canvas API are described on page 225.

Beware

The **\<cite\>** tag should not be used to enclose a person's name.

...element tags cont'd

Don't forget

The values specified by the **<embed>** tag's **width** and **height** attributes need not state the actual dimensions of the resource.

Element:	Description:
<del>	Deleted tag. Encloses text that has been deleted from the document
Attributes:	**cite** – Specifies a URL where an explanation for the deletion is available **datetime** – Specifies the time and date when the deletion was made
<dfn>	Definitive tag. Specifies that the enclosed term is the defining instance of that term
Attributes:	**title** – (global attribute) Specifies the exact value of the term being defined
<div>	Division tag. Encloses a group of other elements for styling purposes only
Attributes:	None
<dl>	Definition List tag. Encloses definition description and definition term tags to create a definition list
Attributes:	None
<dt>	Definition Term tag. Encloses a definition term within a definition list
Attributes:	None
<em>	Emphasis tag. Encloses text that should be displayed in an emphasized manner
Attributes:	None
<embed>	Embed tag. Identifies a resource to be imported into the document Empty element – no closing tag required
Attributes:	**src** – Specifies the URL of a resource **type** – Specifies the resource MIME type **width, height** – Specifies the allocated width and height within the document

...element tags cont'd

Element:	Description:
\<fieldset\>	Fieldset tag. Encloses related form elements to group them together
Attributes:	**name** – Specifies the element's name
\<footer\>	Footer tag. Encloses text providing document information, such as author name, contact details, copyright, etc.
Attributes:	None
\<form\>	Form tag. Encloses one or more form control elements for user input, such as text fields, checkboxes, buttons, etc.
Attributes:	**autocomplete** – Specifies whether the input completion state is "on" or "off" **name** – Specifies a unique form name **action** – Specifies a URL to which the form data is sent upon form submission **method** – Specifies the HTTP method for sending form data to the action URL, as either "GET","POST","PUT" or "DELETE" **enctype** – Specifies the MIME type to be used to encode the form data
\<h1\> \<h2\> \<h3\> \<h4\> \<h5\> \<h6\>	Heading tags. Encloses text to appear as document or section headings, ranked by prominence where **\<h1\>** has the highest rank and **\<h6\>** has the lowest
Attributes:	None
\<head\>	Head tag. Encloses elements that provide information about the document, such as title, meta data, scripts, stylesheets, etc.
Attributes:	None
\<header\>	Header tag. Encloses a document introduction that typically includes a heading element or heading group
Attributes:	None

Hot tip

Typically a document will have just one **\<header\>** element (at the start) and one **\<footer\>** element (at the end).

...element tags cont'd

Hot tip

The top-level **<html>** element is also known as the "root" element.

Element:	Description:
<hgroup>	Headings Group tag. Encloses a number of heading elements, to provide a main heading plus sub-headings
Attributes:	None
<hr>	Horizontal Rule tag. Inserts a horizontal ruled line between differing content Empty element – no closing tag required
Attributes:	None
<html>	HTML tag. Encloses the entire head and body sections of the document
Attributes:	**lang** – (global attribute) Specifies the content language as a short standard abbreviation, such as "en" for English **manifest** – Specifies a URL where the document cache information is available
<i>	Italics tag. Encloses content that is to be displayed in an italic font
Attributes:	None
<iframe>	Inline Frame tag. Inserts a inline framed area containing another document
Attributes:	**src** – Specifies the URL of the document to appear within the inline frame **name** – Specifies a unique frame name **width** – Specifies the frame width **height** – Specifies the frame height

...element tags cont'd

Element:		Description:
\<img>		Image tag. Inserts an image into the document
		Empty element – no closing tag required
	Attributes:	**src** – Specifies the URL of the image
		alt – Specifies a required alternative text description of the image
		width – Specifies the image width
		height – Specifies the image height
		ismap – States that the image is a server-side image map
		usemap – States that the image is a client-side image map
\<input>		Input tag. Inserts an interactive input field that allows the user to enter data
		Empty element – no closing tag required
	Attributes:	**accept** – Specifies an acceptable list of MIME types for file transfer
		alt – Specifies a required alternative text description of an image
		autocomplete – Specifies whether the input completion state is "on" or "off"
		checked – States that a checkbox or radio button should be initially checked
		disabled – Supresses user interaction
		maxlength – Specifies the maximum number of permitted characters
		name – Specifies a unique input name
		readonly – Prevents modification of a text field value by the user
		size – Specifies how many characters can be visible in a text field
		src – Specifies the URL of an image
		type – Specifies the input type, such as "text", "radio", "checkbox", etc.
		value – Specifies a default value for the input, such as a phrase in a text field

Don't forget

The values specified by the **\<img>** tag's **width** and **height** attributes need not state the actual dimensions of the image.

Hot tip

The name and associated value of inputs are sent to a form's action URL upon form submission.

...element tags cont'd

Hot tip

An image-map is a single image with clickable areas that may each have different targets.

Element:	Description:
\<ins>	Inserted tag. Encloses text that has been inserted into the document
Attributes:	**cite** – Specifies a URL where an explanation for the insertion is available **datetime** – Specifies the time and date when the insertion was made
\<kbd>	Keyboard tag. Encloses text that is to be entered by the user from the keyboard
Attributes:	None
\<label>	Label tag. Encloses text that is associated with an input element
Attributes:	**for** – Specifies the ID of the input element to which the text label is to be associated
\<legend>	Legend tag. Encloses text that is a caption for a form fieldset
Attributes:	None
\<li>	List Item tag. Encloses text that is an item in an unordered or ordered list
Attributes:	**value** – Specifies at which number in an ordered list to begin numbering
\<link>	Link tag. Identifies a linked resource Empty element – no closing tag required
Attributes:	**rel** – Specifies the relationship between the document and the linked resource, such as "stylesheet", "icon", etc. **type** – Specifies the resource's MIME type **href** – Specifies the URL of the resource **hreflang** – Advises of the resource language **media** – Advises of the resource media
\<map>	Map tag. Encloses a number of area elements to define an image map
Attributes:	**name** – Specifies a unique map name

Element:	Description:
\<meta\>	Metadata tag. Specifies information about the document defined by its attributes Empty element – no closing tag required
Attributes:	**charset** – Specifies the character encoding used by the document, such as "UTF-8" **content** – Specifies information to be associated with an HTTP header or a name **http-equiv** – Specifies an HTTP header to be associated with the information assigned to the element's content attribute **name** – Specifies a name to be associated with the information assigned to the element's content attribute
\<nav\>	Navigation tag. Encloses anchor elements that provide hyperlinks, to define a navigation section of the document
Attributes:	None
\<noscript\>	No-Script tag. Encloses text to be displayed in the event that JavaScript is not enabled in the web browser
Attributes:	None
\<object\>	Object tag. Inserts an object into the document
Attributes:	**data** – Specifies the URL of the object **type** – Specifies the object's MIME type **name** – Specifies a unique object name **width** – Specifies the object width **height** – Specifies the object height **usemap** – Specifies the URL of a client-side image map to be used by the object
\<ol\>	Ordered List tag. Encloses list item elements to define an ordered list
Attributes:	**start** – Specifies at which number to begin numbering

Hot tip

The **\<object\>** tag may also enclose text to be displayed in the event that the object cannot be inserted.

...element tags cont'd

Beware

The **\<p\>** element should not be used where a more meaningful element can be used.

Element:	Description:
\<optgroup\>	Option Group tag. Encloses related option elements in a drop-down selection list
Attributes:	**label** – Specifies a required group name
\<option\>	Option tag. Encloses text that is an item in a drop-down selection list
Attributes:	**value** – Specifies the value to be sent to the server if the item is selected **selected** – Specifies that the item is initially selected by default **disabled** – Suppresses user interaction
\<p\>	Paragraph tag. Encloses text and automatically adds space before and after itself to create a paragraph block
Attributes:	None
\<param\>	Parameter tag. Specifies runtime plug-in parameters for inserted objects Empty element – no closing tag required
Attributes:	**name** – [Required] Specifies a plug-in parameter name, such as "autoplay" **value** – [Required] Specifies a plug-in parameter value, such as "false"
\<pre\>	Preformatted tag. Encloses text that is to be displayed in a fixed-width font, preserving all spaces and line-breaks
Attributes:	None
\<q\>	Quote tag. Encloses a short quotation, typically within automatically added quote marks
Attributes:	**cite** – Specifies a URL where the origin of the quotation is available

...element tags cont'd

Element:	Description:
\<rp>	Ruby Parentheses tag. Encloses a parentheses character, that will be hidden in browsers that support Ruby annotation
Attributes:	None
\<rt>	Ruby Text tag. Encloses a pronunciation explanation of text within a ruby element
Attributes:	None
\<ruby>	Ruby tag. Encloses text that requires a pronunciation explanation, along with ruby parentheses and ruby text elements
Attributes:	None
\<samp>	Sample tag. Encloses sample output from a computer program
Attributes:	None
\<script>	Script tag. Encloses script code, or specifies an external script resource
Attributes:	**type** – Specifies the script MIME type, such as "text/javascript" (the default) **src** – Specifies the URL of a script file **charset** – Specifies the character encoding used by the document, such as "UTF-8" **defer** – Specifies that an external script will not generate document content, so may be processed after the page loads
\<section>	Section tag. Encloses text that is a section of a document, like a chapter
Attributes:	None

Hot tip

The contents of a **\<samp>** element are typically displayed in a fixed-width font.

...element tags cont'd

Both the **<span>** and **<div>** elements have no structural meaning so are best avoided.

Element:	Description:
<select>	Selection tag. Encloses option elements to define a drop-down selection list
Attributes:	**name** – Specifies a unique list name **size** – Specifies the number of option items that may be visible in the list **multiple** – Specifies that more than one option item may be selected in the list **disabled** – Suppresses user interaction
<small>	Small print tag. Encloses text that is a side comment, such as a legal disclaimer
Attributes:	None
<source>	Source tag. Encloses optional fallback text and specifies a media resource, for audio and video elements
Attributes:	**src** – Specifies the URL of a media file **type** – Specifies the media's MIME type **media** – Specifies the intended viewing medium, such as "all" (the default)
<span>	Span tag. Encloses text for styling purposes only
Attributes:	None
<strong>	Strong tag. Encloses text that should be considered to be important
Attributes:	None
<style>	Style tag. Encloses style rules, to define a stylesheet
Attributes:	**type** – Specifies the stylesheet MIME type, such as "text/css" (the default) **media** – Specifies the intended viewing medium, such as "all" (the default)
<sub>	Subscript tag. Encloses text that is to be displayed as subscript, such as in H_2O
Attributes:	None

...element tags cont'd

Element:	Description:
<sup>	Superscript tag. Encloses text that is to be displayed as superscript, such as in πr^2
Attributes:	None
<table>	Table tag. Encloses table component elements, such the table header, footer, and body elements, to define a full table
Attributes:	None
<tbody>	Table Body tag. Encloses table row and data elements, to define a table body
Attributes:	None
<td>	Table Data tag. Encloses text data that is to be displayed in a regular table data cell
Attributes:	**colspan** – Specifies the number of columns the table data cell should span **rowspan** – Specifies the number of rows the table data cell should span
<textarea>	Text Area tag. Encloses text within a multi-line text input field
Attributes:	**cols** – Specifies the number of characters per line, defining the area width **rows** – Specifies the number of visible rows, defining the area height **readonly** – Prevents modification of the text area content by the user **name** – Specifies a name for the text area **disabled** – Suppresses user interaction
<tfoot>	Table Footer tag. Encloses table row elements to define a table footer section
Attributes:	None

...element tags cont'd

Beware

Don't confuse the **<th>** table heading elements, which define column headings, with the **<thead>** table header elements that define the entire table head section.

Element:	Description:
<th>	Table Heading tag. Encloses text that is to be displayed as a column heading
Attributes:	**colspan** – Specifies the number of columns the heading cell should span **rowspan** – Specifies the number of rows the heading cell should span
<thead>	Table Header tag. Encloses table row elements to define a table header section
Attributes:	None
<title>	Title tag. Encloses text that is the title of the HTML document
Attributes:	None
<tr>	Table Row tag. Encloses table data cell elements, to define an entire table row
Attributes:	None
<ul>	Unordered List tag. Encloses list item elements to define an unordered list
Attributes:	None
<var>	Variable tag. Encloses text that is a mathematical or programming variable
Attributes:	None
<video>	Video tag. Encloses source elements and specifies video media content
Attributes:	**src** – States the URL of the video resource **preload** – Advises of play likelihood **autoplay** – Specifies automatic play **loop** – Specifies automatic replay **controls** – Provides user interface controls **width** – Specifies the video player width **height** – Specifies the video player height

Canvas methods & attributes

The following tables describe the methods and properties available in the Canvas 2D API that allow scripts to draw and paint graphics on a canvas object within an HTML5 document.

Canvas element:	
Methods:	
Getting a canvas context... **var drawing = document.getElementById(" *canvas-id* ") ;** **var context = drawing.getContext("2d") ;** Saving a canvas as an image... ***context*.canvas.toDataURL(" *filename* ") ;**	
Properties:	
***context*.canvas.width** ***context*.canvas.height**	

Hot tip

An exciting Canvas 3D API is expected soon – use your favorite search engine to discover the latest details.

Rectangles:	
Methods:	
Painting a filled rectangle... ***context*.fillRect(*x* , *y* , *width* , *height*) ;** Drawing a stroked rectangle... ***context*.strokeRect(*x* , *y* , *width* , *height*) ;** Removing a rectangular area from the canvas... ***context*.clearRect(*x* , *y* , *width* , *height*) ;**	
Properties:	
None	

Context 2D Object:	
Methods:	
Saving and restoring the canvas state... ***context*.save() ;** ***context*.restore() ;**	
Properties:	
***context*.canvas**	

...canvas cont'd

Hot tip

The script to convert degrees to radians is **r=*degrees**Math.PI/180**.

Colors:

Methods:

Creating a linear gradient fill...
var g = *context*.createLinearGradient(*x0* , *y0* , *x1* , *y1*) ;
g.addColorStop(*offset* , *color*) ;
g.addColorStop(*offset* , *color*) ;
Note: offset values are in the range 0.0-1.0 (start-finish)

Creating a radial gradient fill...
var g = *context*.createRadialGradient(*x0*, *y0*, *r0*, *x1*, *y1*, *r1*) ;
g.addColorStop(*offset* , *color*) ;
g.addColorStop(*offset* , *color*) ;
Note: **r0** and **r1** are radius values in radians, not degrees

Creating a pattern fill...
var pattern = *context*.createPattern(*image* , *repetition*) ;
Note: repetition is **repeat | repeat-x | repeat-y | no-repeat**

Properties:

Name	Possible values	Default
context.**strokeStyle**	*any*	**Black**
context.**fillStyle**	*any*	**Black**
context.**shadowOffsetX**	*floating-point number*	**0.0**
context.**shadowOffsetY**	*floating-point number*	**0.0**
context.**shadowBlur**	*floating-point number*	**0.0**
context.**shadowColor**	*color*	**Transparent-black**

...canvas cont'd

Paths:

Methods:

Creating a path...
context.**beginPath()** ;

Returning to the starting point...
context.**closePath()** ;

Creating a clipping path...
context.**beginPath()** ;
  // **Build the path here.**
context.**clip()** ;

Painting between a path...
context.**fillStyle =** *color* ;
context.**fill()** ;

Drawing along a path...
context.**strokeStyle =** *color* ;
context.**stroke()** ;

Moving the pen...
context.**moveTo(** *x* , *y* **)** ;

Adding a line to a path...
context.**lineTo(** *x* , *y* **)** ;

Adding a rectangle to a path...
context.**rect(** *x* , *y* , *width* , *height* **)** ;

Adding an arc to a path...
context.**arc(** *x* , *y* , *radius* , *start* , *end* , *counterclockwise* **)** ;
Note: **start** and **end** are positions in radians, not degrees
Note: **counterclockwise** will be true or false to set direction

Adding a curve to a path using one control point...
context.**quadraticCurveTo(** *cpx* , *cpy* , *x* , *y* **)** ;

Adding a curve to a path using two control points...
context.**bezierCurveTo(** *cp1x* , *cp1y* , *cp2x* , *cp2y* , *x* , *y* **)** ;

Properties:

None

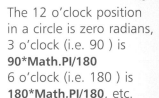

Hot tip

The 12 o'clock position in a circle is zero radians, 3 o'clock (i.e. 90) is **90*Math.PI/180** 6 o'clock (i.e. 180) is **180*Math.PI/180**, etc.

...canvas cont'd

Hot tip

An image object's **width** and **height** properties can be used as arguments in the **drawImage()** method to specify dimensions without knowing the image's actual size.

Text:

Methods:

Painting text...
context.**fillStyle** = *color* ;
context.**fillText(** *textstring* , *x* , *y* , *maxwidth* **)** ;
Note: the **maxwidth** value is optional and may be omitted

Drawing text...
context.**strokeStyle** = *color* ;
context.**strokeText(** *textstring* , *x* , *y* , *maxwidth* **)** ;
Note: the **maxwidth** value is optional and may be omitted

Properties:

context.**font**
Note: Sets size and face, the default is "10px sans-serif"

Images:

Methods:

Creating an image object...
var imageObject = new Image() ;
imageObject.src = " *image-filename* " ;

Drawing an image...
context.**drawImage(** *imageObject* , *x* , *y* **)** ;

Scaling an image...
context.**drawImage(** *imageObject* , *x* , *y* , *width* , *height* **)** ;

Slicing an image...
context.**drawImage(** *imageObject*, **sx,sy,sw,sh, dx,dy,dw,dh)** ;
Note: Arguments specify coordinates and dimensions for both image source and canvas destination

Properties:

imageObject.**width**
imageObject.**height**

Pixels:

Methods:

Read pixel data from the canvas image...
var pixelArray = *context*.**getImageData(** *x, y, width, height* **) ;**

Write pixel data onto the canvas...
context.**putImageData(** *pixelArray* **,** *x* **,** *y* **) ;**

Properties:

pixelArray.**width**
pixelArray.**height**
Note: These are dimensions of the image in the pixel array

pixelArray.**data.length**
Note: This is the element length of the pixels array

Don't forget

Each pixel in a CanvasPixelArray is represented by four elements – one element each for its Red, Green, Blue, and Alpha values.

Lines:

Methods:

(See Paths for line drawing methods)

Properties:

Name	Possible values	Default
context.**lineWidth**	*floating-point number*	1.0
context.**lineCap**	**butt | round | square**	**butt**
context.**lineJoin**	**miter | round | bevel**	**miter**
context.**miterLimit**	*floating-point number*	10

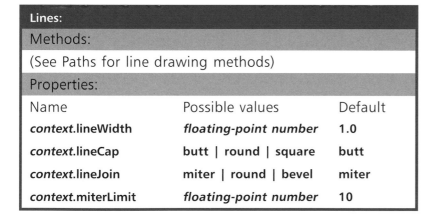

butt   round   square

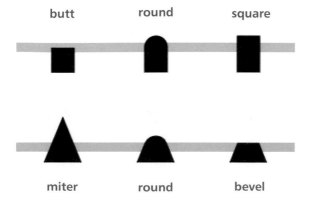

miter   round   bevel

...canvas cont'd

Don't forget

The **transform()** method directly modifies the transformation matrix, which must be reset to its default values after use in order to continue drawing and painting on the canvas as usual.

Transformations:

Methods:

Moving the drawing origin...
***context*.translate(*x* , *y*) ;**
Note: This moves the origin from its <u>current</u> location

Scaling an object...
***context*.scale(*x-factor* , *y-factor*) ;**
Note: The factors scale from the default value of 1.0

Rotating an object...
***context*.rotate(*angle*) ;**
Note: *angle* is a clockwise rotation expressed in radians

Shearing an object along its X-axis...
***context*.transform(1, 0 , *n* , 1, 0, 0) ;**
Note: This directly modifies the transformation matrix by the value supplied as the *n* argument

Shearing an object along its Y-axis...
***context*.transform(1, *n* , 0, 1, 0, 0) ;**
Note: This directly modifies the transformation matrix by the value supplied as the *n* argument

Returning the transformation matrix to its default...
***context*.setTransform(1, 0 , 0, 1, 0, 0) ;**

Properties:

None

Composites:		
Methods:		
None		
Properties:		

context.**globalAlpha**
Note: Sets transparency within the range 0.0 – 1.0

context.**globalCompositeOperation**
Note: Possible acceptable values are...
**source-over | source-in | source-out | source-atop |
destination-over | destination-in | destination-out |
destination-atop | lighter | darker | copy | xor**

Beware

Implementation of all composite operations may not be supported by every web browser.

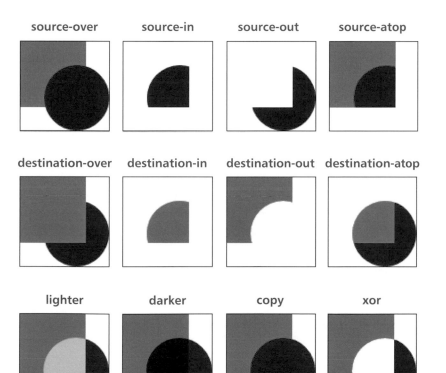

source-over   source-in   source-out   source-atop

destination-over   destination-in   destination-out   destination-atop

lighter   darker   copy   xor

CSS properties & values

Many of the properties used in CSS style rules are listed in the table below. Size values can be specified as pixels with a **px** suffix and colors can be specified as hexadecimal values in the range **#000000** to **#FFFFFF**, or by one of the pre-defined listed names.

Hot tip

Three-figure hexadecimal shorthand values can also be be used for color values. For example, **#0F8** for **#00FF88**.

Property:	Example values:	Specifies:
margin	**5px	10%	auto**	margin size
padding	**5px	10%**	padding size
border	**3px solid black**	border size, type, and color
display	**block	inline**	level type
width	**5px	10%**	width
height	**5px	10%**	height
position	**absolute	relative**	positioning scheme
top	**5px	10%**	distance from top
left	**5px	10%**	distance from left
visibility	**visible	hidden**	show/hide element
overflow	**visible	hidden**	show/hide overflow
color	**red	#FF0000**	foreground color
background	**white	url(tile.png)**	background color or background image
font	**large "Arial", sans-serif**	font size and name
cursor	**pointer	default**	cursor type
text-align	**center	left**	inner text alignment

Don't forget

CSS provides many more properties than those listed here. More comprehensive information is available in "CSS in easy steps".

Color	Hex	Color	Hex
Black	**#000000**	**Green**	**#008000**
Silver	**#C0C0C0**	**Lime**	**#00FF00**
Gray	**#808080**	**Olive**	**#808000**
White	**#FFFFFF**	**Yellow**	**#FFFF00**
Maroon	**#800000**	**Navy**	**#000080**
Red	**#FF0000**	**Teal**	**#008080**
Purple	**#800080**	**Aqua**	**#00FFFF**
Fuchsia	**#FF00FF**	**Blue**	**#0000FF**

Index

D

E

J

K

L

M

N

O

P

Q

R

S

T

U